Brazil and Argentina: From Jungle to Icebergs

Susan Rogers

Published by Pip & Tinks Publishing

ISBN: 978-0-9928634-2-5

This book is dedicated to Antonio Joao Da Silva, the most amazing guide to the Amazon you could ever hope for. Thank you so much Antonio.

ACKNOWLEDGMENT

Thank you Aaron Hendricks (Aaronik Designs) for the front cover design.

Contents

Introduction

This is the second book in the *"Travelling Solo"* series.

The first, *"Vietnam: Journey of unexpected Delights"* was about the holiday where I thought I was joining a tour group, only to find that group consisted of one person – me! After initial wobbles about having nobody to eat with, talk with and share memories with, I accepted my lot and ended up having the most fantastic holiday ever. From that point on, I decided that I wouldn't join a formal tour group again, and indulge in solo travel.

The holiday in Vietnam had happened by accident due to lack of planning on my part and overly trusting the travel agent. With this trip to Argentina and Brazil, I planned ever single bit in advance by myself, learning from mistakes in Vietnam. For example, having ended up in large, impersonal business hotels by accident, this time I specifically chose more traditional hotels where possible. This holiday took place over the period December 2004 and January 2005.

I especially loved the Amazon and to this day it has a special place in my heart.

The Start: December 15th

The holiday really started at Heathrow, where it's fair to say that I was in an excitable and euphoric mood which ironically actually made me somewhat agitated. This was not just because I was about to depart on a great adventure. I phoned Joe on his mobile whilst queuing to check in and was disappointed that it clicked through to voicemail. I left a message saying that I had thought he was going to leave his mobile on in case I wanted to talk to someone at the last minute. Joe had been my partner for four years and we had not only split amicably, but also remained best friends even though he had another partner now. For years I had considered him the brother I never had

I was about to fly off on a fantastic holiday to Argentina and Brazil that I'd been planning for two months, and was looking forward to it with immense anticipation. However, the day previously, I had walked away from paid employment to take the plunge to go solo. Although it had been my decision to take the leap, and despite all the future planning, actually doing so created a wide range of mixed emotions, not least because I was escorted off the premises due to the amount of sensitive information I was privy to. I had always found it slightly amusing when employees who had resigned were marched out of the door, because let's face it, anyone wanting to "steal" sensitive information would have done so before resigning; with memory sticks it was so easy to just copy information from a computer. However as it came to my turn I had felt as guilty as a criminal, even though I hadn't committed any crimes.

1

A deluge of emotions flooded through my veins. Elation at the great escape, sadness that I would no longer be working with my Asian and Latin American colleagues, smugness that I could use my "garden leave salary" to give me a few months cushion, anger at the way I'd been treated over the previous fourteen months, anxiety about the future because going solo was uncharted territory and finally, self-pity because there was nobody to give me a hug; Basically just a whole combination of "stuff" was whirling around my head. I had managed to keep it all in check during the day whilst busying myself with packing and checking last minute arrangements, but now I was at the airport it hit me all of a sudden. In three weeks' time, upon returning from holiday, I would be setting up as a free-lance marketing consultant. The company would be called Rogers International, which sounded very grand but was actually a joke between a friend and myself. I had been planning my next career move for around six months and knew in my bones that I wanted to step out solo, but initially had no clear idea how that would. I had discussed it at length with this friend, who after getting fed up with calling it "Susan's next business move whatever it may be called," shortened it to "Rogers International" because of the amount of business travel I was doing at the time. It eventually stuck and indeed become the company's new name.

I checked in smoothly and went through to departures to pull myself together. I suddenly started chuckling as I recalled the final interview before I was offered the position at the last company. It had been with the chairman, a delightfully down-to-earth chap with whom I bonded instantly and could communicate with easily. The role was a totally new one for ABC: Global Marketing Services

2

Director. They had little idea of what a consumer insight was, no structure for best practice market research and a totally ad-hoc approach to media planning. The role was to raise the standard in all of these areas, introduce and train in best practices globally, recruit and build local teams and create an international community so that key insights could be easily shared. After half an hour chat it was clear that the chairman and I saw eye to eye. He had held up a blank sheet of paper and said in his pronounced Yorkshire accent,

"Susan, this is the job description. You know what we want and need you to do, but you can write whatever you want as long as you achieve the goals." Surely this was my dream job, where I could bring all of my skills from years of working with fast moving consumer goods to this producer of slow moving consumer goods - or in other words, paint.

"I have one final question," the chairman had said with a glint in his eyes and his mouth curling into a grin. "I have no doubt that you can build these teams and move us forward significantly, but how will we know when the goals are met?"

I looked him straight in the face and said, "Once I commit to do something, I throw myself in 110% until I achieve it, so you will know the job is done when I can walk away and everything continues to run smoothly."

I was offered the job there and then, and four years later, I had indeed set up the appropriate best practices globally, built a fantastic international team that could run itself and had made my role undeniably superfluous. The trigger that had caused me to

3

change jobs over the years had started seeping into my bones with increasing intensity over the past nine months, and I'd begun scrabbling around to find work to do, which was a nightmare scenario for me, as I have to be permanently busy. I have never been able to cope well with boredom, especially at work, and when ennui sets in, that was usually a good indicator that it was time to seek pastures new. Instead of looking around for what I called "another big job", I had taken the opportunity to look at the broader picture and what I wanted out of life as a whole, not just work; that had led me to the decision to be self-employed. I could quit with a great sense of pride in the legacy I would leave behind. The original chairman had moved on and another taken his place, and we definitely didn't see things the same way, so I wasn't the least unhappy with the decision. An organisation that centred its strategy on financials and internal health and safety rather than consumer or customer needs, was not an organisation I wanted to remain in. I knew that the Asians wanted me out in Singapore for a broader strategic role, which could have suspended the boredom and given me another year or two, however as much as I loved my Asian colleagues and enjoyed the visits to their regional head quarters in Singapore, I didn't want to work out there permanently, plus I had fallen out of love with the company. The equation of boredom plus dislike, definitely did not equal staying, even though friends and family pointed out that was earning a comfortable wage.

"Surely you can put up with it for another 20 years to get a good retirement package?" one had said. I rest my case.

I had been a round peg in a square hole almost from the beginning, and was something of a rarity, having come in from the "outside" and not being home-grown as many were. Having been plucked from the university milk round, they were still there thirty years later, reluctant to embrace innovative approaches saying in droning voices "we've tried that," or "it won't work," I had achieved all I could in my specific sphere of expertise and it was definitely time to move on before I was sucked into the cloning machine. I was not someone who could sit comfortably in golden handcuffs.

The flight was on time, so I settled down for the long journey. It went pretty smoothly, and I managed to get about seven hours sleep out of a fourteen hours flight, which included an hour at Sao Paulo to drop off and pick up. The only drama was my watch strap snapping when I leaned forward to pluck an in-flight magazine from the pocket in front of me and caught my wrist on the pull out table. Bugger! Still, I could sew it together when I reached Buenos Aires.

I reflected on the major emotional peaks over the past twelve months. My beloved rough collie, Misty, had died six months earlier and I'd recently had my house valued for significantly less than I thought it was worth. However many nice things had also happened. My music had developed enormously (I played the piano accordion) to the point that I was able to start my own band called Sparkies Jazz, named after the new amplified accordion I had treated myself to in the summer. I'd always wished that I could just pick it up and play like Sparky's Magic Piano, and of course amplification = electricity = electrician = sparky, so there was never any doubt what it would be called. I'd made new friends through music, had a great year as chairman of my village social committee, and had organised a marvellous seventieth birthday party for my father at the beginning of the year.

My mind automatically drifted to the launch of Rogers International, then I stopped myself. Frankly all of that could wait until my return. The logo had been designed, the stationery and brochures were at the printers, and the previous week I'd taken the bank manager through my strategic business plan receiving great feedback. There was nothing more to do until my return. I mentally moved the consultancy to the back burner. I had a three-week exciting holiday ahead, which would cross the New Year boundary and blast me into 2005.

Buenos Aires: December 16th

I arrived in Buenos Aires around 10:00. Initially I didn't see anyone with my name on a board, but as I'd been here several times on business I wasn't unduly concerned because I knew the ropes and if the worst came to the worst I could find my own way to the hotel.

However, after standing around for ten minutes I spotted my name on a sign. I waved to the gentleman holding it.

"Buenos días Señorita Rogers. Welcome to Buenos Aires. My name is Alejandro, and I will be looking after your travel arrangements for the next few days." I shook his hand and then he gestured to the door.

"Our car is outside. Please, allow me," he said, and then took charge of the wheelie trolley with my luggage, expertly weaving in and out of the waiting crowds.

"I am in charge of the Argentinean part of your holiday and I want to check all your flight times, transfers, hotels, vouchers and so on when we get to the hotel. I have to say Señorita Rogers, that you are a lot younger than I was expecting."

"How could you estimate my age from a name?" I asked

"Ah, well usually if I pick up a solo lady traveller, she is a little old lady. Younger people seem to travel in groups, pairs or with a partner."

"It's a long story Alejandro," I replied, "but last year I had a holiday in Vietnam and I thought that I was joining a group, but when I arrived there was only person in the group, me."

"However, I had such a fantastic holiday travelling alone, that I decided that it was the only way to travel in the future. So here I am."

On the way to the hotel, he gave me some local information starting with the exchange rate, and warned that people preferred cash to cheques, so if I only had travellers cheques with me, I may find it difficult in some places to cash them. He also told me that the water was safe to drink, but most importantly to be very security conscious all the time, as I was in a relatively poor country and theft was not uncommon. If I stuck to the main tourist areas I should be okay but I had to be really careful if I decided to wander outside of these.

I recalled visiting *La Boca* area of Buenos Aires during a business trip. It was the old waterside area that had been completely run down until the sixties, when an artist had painted the buildings in numerous shades of bright, vibrant colours; now it was a rampant tourist trap, with cafes, over-priced souvenir shops and pavement artists. People danced tango in the street with local experts willing to give tourists a turn around the flag stones in exchange for a lucrative tip. You had to be on your guard here for hawkers and hustlers, and of course everything was obscenely overpriced. Just a few blocks away was the famous *La Bombonera* football ground, but beyond that lay the dark areas of poverty stricken Buenos Aires. Those were the areas that unless you were familiar with them, you avoided.

Alejandro pointed out that I didn't look Argentinean and therefore made an obvious target. I didn't really need to be told this after being robbed in Budapest just three weeks earlier during a business trip. I had always thought that I was extremely security conscious, but my strategy had been foiled by the nimble fingered gypsy waifs of Hungary. As the experience was still a little raw, I had taken extra precautions for this holiday. I was carrying little cash and had three credit cards hidden in three different places. I could never get on with hidden money belts as regardless of the material they all seem to chaff or come undone and slide down my trouser leg at some point, so I had taken my small back-pack rather than a handbag, My purse was at the bottom of the largest compartment, which meant that a thief would have to work past a jumper, guide books, toilet paper and packets of sweets before reaching the wallet, by which time I'd like to think that I'd have felt someone there. Finally Alejandro told me to be patient with flights and internal travel because frequently plans change or flights were cancelled and it was a case of *que sera*, so there was no point in getting upset or angry about it.

There were pangs of nostalgia for the ex-company, only because I'd always experienced great trips out here and thoroughly enjoyed working with my enthusiastic Latin American colleagues, but what made it worse was that the hotel I was in, *Loi Suites Recoletas*, was next door to where I usually stayed on business and my room also had a view over the Recoleta cemetery which was an almost

9

identical vista to previous visits. However the beautiful white gateway to the cemetery, which seemed to change colour with the light of the day was now brilliant white, and I couldn't recall ever seeing it look so resplendent.

The receptionist oozed with charm and politeness and the check-in was a smooth process. I sat down with Alejandro to go through the details of my documents. The first discrepancy we found was about the flight the next day. My ticket was for an hour earlier than his itinerary showed; oops! He said he'd check it out and give me a call later at the hotel.

I tried to change a traveller's cheque but was told that the hotel will only change cash so I changed £40 sterling. I hoped that this wouldn't be a problem everywhere as I'd mainly taken travellers cheques, but with this occurrence and Alejandro's warning, I could be facing difficulties. There was no paper-work so I had no idea whether I was being ripped off or not. It seemed a bit of a coincidence that the exchange rate was dead on four dollars to the pound. The currency was really Pesos, but since the devaluation a couple of years earlier, the locals now referred to them as dollars.

The room was simple but very pleasant. It was one room with a double bed, a small settee with a colourful throw over it and a small kitchenette area with a microwave and coffee maker.

Deciding that I needed to get out and get some fresh air after the long journey, I changed into shorts, a vest and flip flops and wandered off to find a corner shop where I could get a bottle of water and some milk. The sun was already beating down at around

80 degrees and just changing into holiday gear lifted my spirits. There was something very liberating about shorts and flip-flops. Following the Vietnam holiday where I'd found it virtually impossible to get a decent cup of coffee outside of the hotels, I came prepared for this vacation with two plastic pouches with me, one with caffeinated coffee and the other with de-caf. I ought to hold my hand up here and say that I am an absolute coffee plebeian, generally preferring instant to the real beans. Yes, I enjoy the occasional ground coffee, but for daily consumption, instant does me just fine.

I returned with a litre of milk and half a dozen small bottles of water and checked out the hotel pool which to my horror was covered by a plastic ceiling. I didn't want to sit under a plastic ceiling. I wanted to be out and about feeling real rays of sun on my body, mingling with the locals and taking in the ambience. I decided the best way to spend the first afternoon of the holiday was to sit in the park outside the cemetery and read an easy holiday book to clear my mind of other more important things. I needed, and wanted, to wind down and make the most of this holiday; a slobby afternoon without any sightseeing would suit me down to the ground. I knew this area pretty well from my business trips so there wasn't the same urge to get out and explore that I'd usually have, just a great half-day to chill and take in the familiar surroundings.

I had visited the cemetery during my last business trip when there were no meetings in the afternoon and my flight wasn't until the evening. It is allegedly one of the world's most beautiful cemeteries and was like a city in its own right. A city for the dead. I would add it to anyone's itinerary while visiting Buenos Aires.

The cemetery contains hundreds of elaborate mausoleums constructed in a broad range of architectural styles, many fashioned in marble and adorned with decorative emblems and statues. It is easy to navigate around the entire burial ground is laid out in square sections like a city block, with wide tree-lined main streets intersected by narrower lanes. It must be down to the families to maintain the individual mausoleums, as some were immaculate-gleaming white with large vases of freshly picked flowers, whereas others were dirty and scuffed and clearly hadn't been visited for several years. Sadly some were even worse with rolled up crisp packets and sandwich wrappings poked into nooks and crannies or flung over the small gated walls. Although breathtaking it is also eerily quiet to walk around the cemetery with the enormous mausoleums towering forebodingly over you. It is not surprising that it contains the graves of eminent people.

To the non-Argentinean visitor the most famous person resting there is probably Eva Perón buried in the Duarte family tomb. It was to the chagrin of the higher echelons of society that she is buried here at all, although it was many years after her death that she was entombed here. It is a very simple and modest affair compared with its neighbours and is set down one of the side streets so I would suggest you buy a map before visiting. I didn't the first time I was there and it took me ages to find the tomb. Other notables buried here include Argentinean presidents and generals, Nobel Prize winners and other elites of their day.

I walked past the elaborate entrance for the cemetery and into the park which had scores of little craft stalls along the pathways

12

mainly selling jewellery, leather goods, paintings and other objet d'art. A thin leather necklace caught my attention and I tried it on. It was only fifteen pesos, around one pound sterling, and I hadn't brought any jewellery with me, so I treated myself.

I found a sunny spot in the gardens and settled down on the freshly mown lawn with a book, the second *Bridget Jones's Diary*, nice and easy reading to chill the brain cells.

There was a brilliant blue sky without a cloud in sight and the temperature had soared to the mid-eighties with a very pleasant light breeze ensuring that it didn't feel too hot. After a couple of hours in the sun, and with the appetising smell of cooking wafting from the food stalls - a mixture of savoury meat nibbles and sweet pancakes, I definitely felt a little peckish. I was torn between wanting to try several of the delicacies on offer but equally conscious that I was saving myself for a delicious, juicy Argentinean beef steak in the evening. Unable to totally avoid the beckoning smells I decided on a compromise: a little al fresco bar where I ordered a local beer and a platter of nibbles before carrying on reading.

I looked around at the people sitting at the other tables. La Recoleta is the wealthy chic area of Buenos Aires. There were a lot of old women sitting either alone or in pairs. They looked as if they had come from bygone days and were determinedly clinging onto the past. They were very well dressed, dripping in jewellery and had painted eyebrows giving them an Édith Piaf look. There was a sort of arrogant pride on their faces as if to say that they were still living in the great days of economic wealth. I could imagine them living in an apartment with only two tins of beans in the kitchen cupboard, yet showing defiance when out in public.

There were a few men around as well. I'd noticed on business trips here that they Argentineans are an exceedingly handsome race; the older they were, the better looking they became. Many of them were grey-haired, even the forty years olds, but this added a distinguished look to their already handsome and well chiselled features. It was definitely a pleasure people-watching here and to this day I maintain that Buenos Aires is one of the best places in the world to embark on such an occupation.

After my snackette I realised that I'd been sitting in the direct sunlight for about four hours and it was time to retreat. I headed back to the hotel for a long soak in the bath and to begin writing my diary as well as mentally preparing for my steak. I had no doubts that I would be eating beef that evening, and indeed the next evening and probably the evening after also. The meat in Argentina was quite simply the best I'd ever tasted and I intended to make the most of it. Perhaps I could even fool myself into believing I had been on an Atkins diet for three weeks!

I had already caught the sun and my shoulders were not only decidedly red but also feeling a little sore. I hadn't faced much sun exposure in recent months, even with my business travelling, so I had been paler than usual. As I rarely burn in the sun I had let my guard down a little too much that afternoon.

However, it was not just my shoulders that were a little bit sore as I had managed to blister three toes under the hot water tap. I had turned on what I thought was the cold bath tap and stuck my foot under the jet of water just to check. Ouch! Not only was it the hot tap but it must have been close to boiling point.

After suitably soaking and refreshing myself I headed out to find a restaurant. There was no doubt whatsoever that I was absolutely spoilt for choice. I chose one that looked a little basic but it had good lighting, so I'd be able to sit and read my book, and the menu was enticing. It turned out to be a bad choice as the meal was average and the steak not up to expectations.

Back at the hotel I listened to some of the CDs I had taken with me. Although I had a walkman with me the room had a mini CD player, so I used that. I listened to some compilations that I had recorded specifically for the trip. My will included individual letters that were to be sent out to friends but because of the increasing importance of music in my life I had supplemented the letters with discs of music that were appropriate for each person. Listening to the music made me feel less far away.

I picked up my e-mails and there was a really funny message from Joe.

Susan's itinerary for 16th December:

"...Along with Rio de Janeiro and São Paulo, Buenos Aires is the most cosmopolitan city in South America. There are plenty of museums and galleries to visit as well as the old immigrant district of La Boca with its multi-coloured houses and history of Tango. The central part of town is home to the colonial heartland, government buildings, churches, the chic shopping districts with their run-down

15

Parisian aspect, and the bohemian area, San Telmo where quaint old houses are interspersed with antique shops, tango bars and expensive restaurants..."

Joe's itinerary for 16th December:

"...Saltdean (the ex-home of a Butlin's holiday camp): beans on toast, play on the computer, moan about the cold, do the washing-up, watch the telly, fall asleep for two hours ..."

I burst out laughing. It was so typical of Joe's sense of humour.

Alejandro phoned me spot on 22:00 as promised to confirm that my pick up would be 13:00 the next day. No need to set an alarm. I drifted off to sleep whilst listening to the CDs.

Iguazu: December 17th

I was awake at around 06:30 and it wasn't a bad night's sleep. The first night in a strange hotel usually guarantees restlessness, as the noises, smells and unfamiliar bed sheets are all alien, but I was out like a light and slept right through.

I made some coffee and ran a bath. Oh dear. I realised I'd managed to block the toilet. I hadn't used it to the extent that it should be blocked so this was quite a surprise and I seemed to make things worse whilst trying to clear it. I thought that perhaps it would drain away whilst I had breakfast so I left it and headed downstairs.

Breakfast was average with a small selection of fruits and breads but at least it got me going for the day. After returning to the room I could see that the toilet had still not sorted itself out and I suspected that the previous occupant must have blocked it at some point. I gave it one further flush; willing it to clear like magic with the extra surge of water but it didn't, and instead came perilously close to overflowing. The only thing to do was to now leave it and tell reception on the way out.

I went for another walk around the gardens surrounding La Recoleta Cemetery mesmerised by the colourful craft stalls that were already trading. I needed to buy a lightweight T-shirt as all the tops I had brought with me were either sleeveless vests for the sun or long sleeved for the evenings. I had one short sleeved polo shirt but the material was too thick for the heat. My shoulders glowed like

17

Belisha beacons from the previous day's sun and I knew I would have to keep them covered for the next couple of days.

It was always lovely strolling through La Recoleta gardens, especially early morning when the artisans were setting up their stalls, carefully placing each item on the table with the love afforded to such beautiful crafts. As there were not many potential customers around at that time of the day they had the opportunity to say good morning, ask me where I was from and wish me a fantastic holiday. It was almost impossible to imagine in such a beautiful area that I was in the same city as some definite no-go areas. However, I found that I kept checking my bum bag to make sure that nobody had nicked the few notes that I had brought out with me. In the hotel room that morning I'd kept sharing out my money amongst different hiding places in my luggage. I was being a little paranoid after the Budapest experience, but equally I kept telling myself that just because you are paranoid, doesn't mean that they are not out to get you. It crossed my mind that I may get home to find that I had loads of Pesos secreted away that I'd forgotten about during the holiday; though as long as they were not in shorts pockets when I put them in the washing machine then it was not that big a deal.

I noticed a money changing kiosk and I stopped to see if they would change traveller's cheques.

"Buenos días. Puedo cambiar los cheques de viaje aquí?" I said in my slow Spanish.

"Yes, certainly senorita, but I prefer cash. You have dollars?"

"I'm afraid not, just traveller's cheques."

18

"OK, but I charge an additional three dollars per transaction."

"Thanks, I'll be back in five minutes."

After Alejandro's warning and the difficulty at the hotel the previous evening, I thought it best to change some cheques whilst I had the opportunity to do so. I collected £50 of traveller's cheques and returned to the kiosk. Although the trader was pleasant enough I could tell that cheques were his least favourite transaction. As if reading my mind he said,

"I have to send the cheques to my bank. They have to send them to America. It sometimes takes many weeks before I see my money again."

I smiled apologetically but felt there was nothing more I could say. I returned to the hotel to finish packing, not that I had unpacked much as there wasn't really a need to do so for a one-night stay. The damned toilet was still blocked. I had to go down to reception to use the facilities in the foyer. I repeated to the receptionist that my toilet was still blocked. She smiled and threw her hands in the air,

"The toilets, they are always blocking. Poor drains. It will be mended soon."

I checked out and waited for Alejandro to arrive. I finished reading my first book and left it in the room so that it could be added to the hotel's selection of English language books for guests. I had taken The Last Juror, John Grisham's latest novel out of the suitcase and added it to my day bag for the flight, but decided instead to gen up on Iguazu for when I got there. I only had one full

19

day, and two half-days planned for the Falls and I wanted to see them from the Brazilian and Argentinean sides.

Alejandro arrived early and then proceeded to count his money in front of me.

"Excuse me Suzanne, but I do not trust banks. Nobody in Argentina trusts banks since the last crisis. We had a great depression from 1998 until 2002. It was very scary. You would go to your bank and discover that the government had taken your money. They left a sort of IOU, but basically you couldn't get hold of your own money. How were we to live?"

"I know," I added, "I used to come here on business trips and one time, the lady I was meeting with told me that hardly any work was being done in the office as people were checking their bank accounts online every half hour to make sure that their money was still there. My friend had been saving up for many years to buy a new apartment, and she was petrified she would lose the money. She was lucky that hers was never taken, but it was frozen and she could only take out $250 a week."

"Yes, I remember that so well," sighed Alejandro, "I had to queue for ages to get to the cash point as everyone was taking out $250 each week even if they didn't need it as they felt that they had more control over their money if it was in their house and not the bank! $250 dollars a week might sound like quite a lot of money, but you had to pay for everything from that, including rent as landlords stopped accepting cheques, and everything had to be paid for with cash."

"My friend found it difficult because she had to pay for childcare so she and her husband could go to work, but the carer was paid cash, and after she had been given her weekly wage there was little left for food and fuel. I also know there was a lot of rioting. I was here at the end of 2001 and although I didn't actually see anything security was a lot tighter than usual, and the TV was reporting riots just a few blocks away."

He continued to tell me that he didn't trust banks, so as soon as he got some money in pesos, his wages or tips for example, he changed it to US dollars and then hid them in his house. He proceeded to sort his money into piles of equal denominations and then counted out about four hundred dollars in front of me. Whilst doing this he half muttered to himself, and half to me, that he was not a rich man, but comfortable and he lived alone. He managed to drop into the conversation several times that he lived alone.

"I used to have an English wife but she went off with my neighbour, doh! So I keep my money in cash otherwise she'd get her hands on it. Did I tell you that I now live alone?"

"Yes, you did." I smiled. I thought that maybe he had a soft spot for me, but the feeling was not mutual.

He asked me how I was finding the hotel and I said that it was fine, but I'd unfortunately managed to block the toilet. He just shrugged and said "They've got plumbers."

He had reconfirmed my flight with three different people and triple-checked the time of departure. He also confirmed that he would see me on the 31st when I would briefly pass through Buenos

Aires again on my way to Patagonia. The car arrived and we set off for the airport. This time it was to the national airport and not the international one. It was the first time that I had been there and it was a lovely terminal, quite small, but new and clean and the check-in was impressively fast. Alejandro saw me to the departure door and then said,

"Suzanne, we have a new rule. When you arrive back at Buenos Aires you are to stay in the airport. You are not to go outside, and you stay inside until I arrive. Maybe I am a little late, but I will be there. I am responsible for you when you are in Argentina." I agreed, shook his hand and went through to the departure lounge.

There was plenty of time before the flight as Alejandro had not wanted to risk being held up in the traffic nor have other obstacles cause a delay. I was feeling a little peckish as it was now about 13:30 so I took a seat in the café. It wasn't a very inspiring menu, but I tried to order a pizza. It was off the menu. Never mind. I ordered a burger and chips instead. It was served with the flimsiest plastic cutlery I'd ever come across: both the knife and fork bent almost in half when I pierced the burger. Airports were now only using plastic cutlery because of the potential to use the metal versions as dangerous weapons. Unfortunately, the chips were extremely crispy; not only were they totally impenetrable by flimsy plastic forks, but they would catapult halfway across the café when the implements were tried on them. When I realised that there was a carpet of chips forming around my table, I reverted to using my fingers to eat. At least it would be impossible to use this cutlery for any dangerous activities. At a push, the knife may just be able to spread jam.

The flight was only an hour and twenty minutes and the airport at Iguazu is charming. Small, provincial and friendly. The luggage didn't take too long to arrive, and then I was out of the airport to meet my second guide, Ciro. He was a small thin Argentinean who looked as if he was wearing clothes a size too big for him. He had a well-worn leathery face which sported a thin greying moustache over his pinched lips and he beamed a smile that almost looked too large for his face. He grasped my hand with both of his and I noticed that his finger and thumb were stained a dark nicotine orange.

"Welcome Miss Rogers, welcome," he said enthusiastically as he shook my hand. "I am Ciro and I will be looking after your travel arrangements for the next two days. Come, the driver is outside ready to take us to the hotel. Allow me please." With that he took charge of the luggage trolley and marched towards the exit.

On the way to the hotel he showed me a map of the Falls,

"Miss Rogers, I suggest that the best thing for you, is to do the Argentinean side tomorrow at your own pace and then, if you are up for it, an early start on Sunday morning and we cover the Brazilian side en route to the airport."

"Yes, that sounds great," I said enthusiastically, "and please call me Susan."

"However," he added, "there is a fee to see the falls in Brazil. It will be $40."

Wow, that was quite a fee but I was only going to be here once in my lifetime, so it was worth it.

"Yes, okay," I replied, not quite as enthusiastic as before.

"I think it will take you a whole day to see the Falls from the Argentinean side." he said. "There are about ten kilometres of walkways, and then also a boat trip where you get soaked going under the Falls. The boat trip will cost you a further $25 dollars I'm afraid, but it is good for you to see and feel the Falls up close. It is better that you do the boat trip in the afternoon, because it is so hot during the day, about 95 degrees, that you will be very glad to have a cold shower in the afternoon." He said laughing at his own humour. "Believe me Suzanne, you will get totally soaked in the boat. I mean, totally soaked. It is better at the end of the day when you are ready to return to the hotel."

We arrived at the hotel and after checking in Ciro bid me farewell and said he would see me early Sunday morning. The hotel looked really pleasant, although a little shabby as if it were a couple of years overdue a coat of paint. It was the Sheraton, and the only hotel within the Iguazu national park, which is why I had chosen it. I threw back the curtains in my room and gasped as I realised I had a view of the Falls. In the distance I could see part of the top of the Falls with white spray clouding around the waterfall. I opened the sliding door to the balcony and could instantly hear them. I must have been about a mile away from the Falls, yet their pounding on the rocks was unmistakable.

I made a cup of coffee with my travel kettle adding powdered milk. I didn't especially like Marvel powdered milk, but had discovered that if you make it into milk rather than adding it directly to the cup of prepared coffee, it tastes a little better.

There were no spoons in the hotel room, just little spatula things from the minibar to mix your drinks with; it took about twenty spatulas of coffee and ten of Marvel just to make one small cup. I was tempted to try and pour direct from the plastic food bags of coffee into the cup, but I knew from past experience with bags of compost that when you tip, nothing comes out, then you give it a little help and the whole lot comes whizzing out at once. I didn't want to lose my supplies so early in the holiday, nor did I want to leave traces of suspicious looking white powder all over the place.

It was about 16:00 and the day wasn't over yet: I could have some exercise and do the upper walk of the Falls before dinner.

The national park has walkways through the jungle leading to the Falls, all clearly marked, and, as Ciro had told me, it was impossible to get lost.

There were not many people around, so it was incredibly tranquil, and my spirits were lifted well before I reached the Falls.

Wow. Stunning. Awesome. I ran out of superlatives to describe the Iguazu Falls. I took what must have been well over a hundred photos with the camera, but also a fair bit of movie footage as I wanted to capture the rush of the water in movement and noise. I wanted to be able to relive this experience over and over again. It was just so magical. I don't think that I fully appreciated photographs of the Falls before I came on holiday: it hadn't really dawned on me that Iguazu is made up of about three hundred waterfalls depending on the amount of rainfall. The sheer size and force of the Falls was astounding. There were also permanent rainbows. Beautiful, strong vibrant rainbows, a whole one, but lots of sections as well. I reckoned that I'd probably just seen more rainbows in two hours than I had in the rest of my life put together. I made a wish on each rainbow - although some were the same because I ran out of wishes before I ran out of rainbows. I was extremely excited at the prospect of spending a whole day amongst the Falls the next day.

Back at the hotel, I couldn't decide whether to have a shower or go and eat. My stomach won. I bought my first batch of postcards and wrote brief messages whilst downing a lovely chilled beer.

I changed another traveller's cheque whilst I had the opportunity, the rate was awful, but I needed the cash to pay for my tours the next day. Indeed, everything in this hotel was expensive, but they had a captive audience as it was the only one inside the national park and there were no towns within spitting distance, so you paid through the nose. A small bottle of water in the room was over £1.

There were two restaurants. One was a la Carte and the other a buffet. Clearly the buffet would be the cheaper option so I headed in that direction. To get to the buffet room you had to walk through the a la carte restaurant. This restaurant had a harpist playing, creating a romantic and relaxing atmosphere. The cheap, or rather cheaper, restaurant was teeming with kids so there was no choice really and I opted for the a la carte.

It didn't bother me eating in romantic settings. Since Vietnam and after loads of business trips where I'd eaten alone in goodness knows how many restaurants with soft romantic background music I'd become used to it. Anyway, I had my book to read whilst dining.

I elected to order steak after the disappointment the previous night, and this one was much better. It wasn't quite up to the "usual" Argentinean standard, that is the best in the world, but it wasn't bad and definitely an improvement from the previous evening. I was also served with a complimentary Margarita. I generally don't like most spirits but It's one of the few cocktails that I absolutely love. I had a great recipe for Margaritas back home, but I hadn't made one for years and had forgotten just how tangy and delicious they were with the salted rim of the glass and sharp lime kick.

Returning to the room, I tried to find an English-speaking TV channel to catch up on the news. There were forty six channels and only one, a movie channel, was in English. No BBC World News. The TV menu purported to have CNN, but the reception was so bad that it was virtually non-existent. I wouldn't have known whether I'd got CNN, The Discovery Channel or Cartoon network.

Giving up on the TV, I read some more of my book whilst listening to CDs before drifting off to sleep.

Waterfall shower: December 18th

I was down for breakfast at around 07:30, and despite being in a reasonable hotel, I could only describe it as average at best. I had quite fancied having some bacon and eggs to set me up for the day, but the bacon smelt decidedly dodgy, so I chose ham, cheese and bread instead.

I returned to my room to prepare my day bag. Ciro had warned me that I would get very wet. If I decided to do the boat trip, I would be drenched. I wrapped my cameras in plastic bags and then just to be on the safe side, wrapped them again in a laundry bag.

Looking out of the window I could still hardly believe the stunning view. Each time I looked out, the Falls seem to get closer as if they were drawing me to them. I saw a monitor lizard crossing the lawn and turned to grab the movie camera, but by the time I had it out of the laundry bag, turned it on and focused it, the lizard had disappeared behind a tree. Drat!

I flung my backpack on and headed out as an intrepid traveller, deciding that my first port of call would be the area of the Falls called The Devil's Throat. To get to this, I had to walk through the jungle to a train stop, which would then take me to the beginning of the walking platforms, along which I'd be able to view the spectacular falls from above. As I arrived, a train pulled away. The guard asked me what I wanted and I pointed to the disappearing train.

"Sorry señorita, but the next one is in half an hour." I backtracked to the little station kiosk, bought a bottle of water, which was only marginally cheaper than at the hotel, found a bench and sat down to wait. Who cared about having to wait? It was a beautiful day with clear blue skies and the sun dancing on the stunning flora around me. I had my camera out, ready and waiting to capture any more creatures I may be lucky to spot. I didn't see any of note other than small chirpy birds that darted from one branch to the next much faster than I could capture on the camera.

The train arrived and it was charming. A rickety, wooden open-sided affair offering a most pleasant ten-minute ride through the jungle. After leaving the train, I was at the start of the walk to the Devil's Throat. It was about a mile along a purpose-made wooden walkway that alternated between jungle and over the water. The pounding of the Falls became louder with each step and as I crossed the last walkway leading to the Devils Throat's viewing point spray was tinkling down, well before I got close. When I arrived at the viewing point, I was nothing short of stunned. The sheer weight and volume of water cascading down was quite incredible and it had to be seen, heard and felt: I knew instantly that none of the photos could ever do it justice. The video may give a better feel, but not the full depth considering the sheer size, nearly three hundred feet deep, five hundred feet wide and the total horseshoe shape of this Garganta del Diablo being nearly half a mile in length. It was just too much to take in. The amount of spray created by these incredible torrents of extremely fast-moving water made it impossible to see further than a few feet into the throat, and I could very clearly understand why this mass of exploding water

30

was so named. This monster was formed by about half the water of the Falls being forced through a relatively narrow channel and it just seemed to suddenly disappear from the flat river above.

I returned along the walkway and caught the next train back to the start. I then had a decision to make. I could do the Lower Falls walk or go on the boat trip. As the boat trip ended at the bottom of the lower walks, I concluded that it was best to do the boat trip first, and then as I walked back up to the top I'd cover all the Lower Falls.

I made my way to where the "water adventure" started and produced my ticket. I was trying to speak Spanish, yet all the vocabulary I was searching for was just not in my brain. I had been having one-to-one Spanish lessons at work and, therefore, I learned very quickly; but like with anything, you learn it quickly and then forget it quickly. My lessons had also been hampered when we had moved to a ridiculous open-plan office layout, without sufficient meeting rooms. Since secretaries block booked the rooms with spuriously invented meetings, there was never a guaranteed quiet space where I could continue my Spanish.

The girl at the counter asked if I was English. I said yes, and explained in slow Spanish that I was just learning Spanish and could only speak a little, but that it was important I tried when I could. The girl at the counter was brill and instead of trying to talk to me in English, she slowed her Spanish down for the conversation.

"Buenos dias señorita, y en qué puedo ayudarle?" I paused and then asked about the time of the next boat trip slowly, stumbling

31

over some of the words but determined to ask in Spanish. "Cuánto tiempo antes de que comience la próxima viaje en barco?"

""Viente cinqo minutos senorita."

"Twenty five minutes?" I responded in English just to be certain, and she smiled and nodded.

"Hasta la vista," I replied, using probably the one Spanish phrase that everyone knows, regardless of whether or not they have had Spanish lessons.

There was a café close by and although it was only 11:30, I thought it best to get a sandwich here because I didn't know how long the water trip was going to take or whether there would be food available during the rest of the walk. I confidently ordered, "Una sandwich de jamon crudo y un boteille de agua por favor". He understood that I wanted a ham sandwich, but then I tried to say "without butter," but for the life of me could not remember what the Spanish for butter was, and he didn't speak any English so had no comprehension of the word "butter". I reached for my dictionary only to discover that I'd brought the phrase book instead. I quickly thumbed to the pages covering restaurant phrases, but none had the word butter in them. There was a small dictionary section at the back but again, "butter" was not there. I shrugged as if to say okay, I'll take whatever comes. I carried on studying the "eating out section" of the phrase book, and about a nanosecond before the sandwich arrived I found the word. I grinned at the chap,

"Mantequilla! Sin mantequilla. No mantequilla. No butter por favor."

He lifted the edge of the sandwich and I could see there was no butter in it anyway, still I had learned a new word that would be etched in my mind for the rest of the holiday, if not forever.

The sandwich came with a napkin that had the texture of Izal toilet paper, except wafer thin and the same absorbency as a piece of greaseproof paper. After eating the sandwich I wiped my mouth and the serviette disintegrated like rice paper and stuck to my face. Not having a mirror on me I stood there, much to the amusement of the family on the next table, as I tried peeling the remaining paper off my face.

The water adventure started by being loaded into a huge open-top old military lorry and taken for an eight kilometres journey further upstream. That was quite an adventure in itself, after climbing up and plonking myself on the seat I leapt up again rapidly as it must have been about 100 degrees. The seats had a chipped plastic covering and I was wearing shorts. Having burnt my legs, I pulled out a sarong from my day bag and placed that on the seat first. We rattled along unmade roads through the jungle, and I was willing one of the small bears known to inhabit the area to trundle across the road, but although it was a pleasant, but bumpy, ride, and I enjoyed the leafy vaulted ceiling of lush green branches, no bears were seen.

We arrived at the embarkation point and I climbed into one of the two large speedboats. They were giant dinghies, each holding about 20 people, and we had to put life vests on. We were each given a plastic bag for our personal belongings that we wished to keep dry. It was too small for me to stuff the backpack in so I pulled out my

Sheraton laundry bag and used that instead. It's fair to say that I am NOT a water person and indeed have never been keen on water activities and I doubt I ever would be. Putting a life jacket on convinced me that we would topple over at some point.

Then suddenly we were off. Very fast. On the flat smooth river, the captain weaved around, doing turns at 45 degrees to give us a bit of a thrill as that's what he thought the tourists wanted; I actually found it good fun even though I had the feeling that if he were to lean the boat a further 5 degrees I'd be in the water. But of course, he made this trip several times a day and he was in absolute control of the manoeuvres. Surprisingly, I found it extremely exhilarating speeding along with the wind and spray from the water in my face, and could understand for the first time why people enjoyed water sports so much.

After several minutes on the smooth glassy water we reached an area of rocky rapids, and I was extremely impressed with the captain's ability to weave in and out of these at the same speed as before without beaching the boat anywhere. Before I knew it, we had reached the bottom of the Falls and the boat stopped so that we could take some pictures. There was of course a photographer on board should we want a nice souvenir to take back and, for a moment, I was tempted because I hardly ever get any pictures of myself on holiday, but he wanted something horrendous like £10, so I passed my camera to the lady behind me and asked her to take a shot.

Once everyone had taken all the pictures they wanted, the boat left this first part of the Falls and went round the corner slowly and

34

carefully. We were now at the foot of the Devil's Throat and the water thundered down from the rocks like a giant plughole. We stopped again for photos and then the Captain shouted "Poner la cámara en el bolso. Please, cameras in bags." After glancing around to check that everyone had their bags stowed away he revved up the boat, swung it around and took us straight into one of the Falls. We were not talking "a bit of spray" here, and indeed we were not talking "a splash from the Falls", but we were talking total immersion. It was like being suddenly plunged under a freezing cold power shower on full blast. The captain manoeuvred the boat forwards and backwards to ensure that we all got a real good soaking. After the shock of the initial surge hitting us, it was quite good fun. After a couple more "showers" we returned to the decking platform.

Back on dry land, I realised that I hadn't been as smart as I thought I'd been taking just the plastic laundry bag. I should also have taken a change of clothes or at the very least my flip-flops. I was absolutely soaked through to my underwear. I wrung out my vest and shorts but my trainers were like wearing a pair of sponges. The other tourists squelched off to the open-topped lorry for the return journey, but as I was going to walk back to the hotel via the Lower Falls walk I headed off along a marked path. I started the ascent to the top of the Falls, and my shoulders were starting to burn from the sun. There was only one thing for it, so I took my vest off and draped it around my shoulders to protect them. It was now pretty obvious that I was wearing a bra and not a bikini top, but what the hell, I couldn't see any other people walking the trail and, if worse came to worst and someone saw me I wouldn't see them ever again once I'd left the Falls, so it was unlikely to become one of life's major embarrassments.

The walk back was fantastic. Around each corner was another waterfall, with spray and rainbows dancing in the sunshine. I was surprised that Iguazu didn't hold the accolade for being the biggest waterfall in the world, but when I checked my travel guide later, it failed this because it was counted as lots of smaller waterfalls, even though they all poured into the same river. I didn't care, it was certainly the most wondrous Falls I had ever visited, and until I had arrived I just hadn't fully comprehended their size. I had been right, no picture would do them justice.

I squelched my way back to the hotel. Once in my room I caught sight of myself in the mirror. Oh no! My arms and lower neck were brown or red, and the rest of my body was flabby and lily white. I must have looked a right sight clambering up to the top of the Falls. Oh well, as I had said to myself earlier, I wouldn't be seeing anyone from around here again.

It was time to chill out a bit as I'd covered a fair few miles, some of it on quite steep terrain, and I also needed to get the bits of my body brown that were currently porcelain coloured. I stripped down to my underwear, hung the wet clothes on the balcony to dry and did a spot of topless sun bathing. Unfortunately the heat was such that I only managed about half an hour, so I retreated inside to catch up with the diary and to send some emails.

It was a real pleasure sitting there writing. The view over the Falls was tranquil, inspirational and calming, and I felt that I could write and write forever.

There were definitely lots of benefits in taking a small, lightweight laptop on holiday. Firstly, I could type up the diary as I went, unlike the Vietnam adventure which I wrote long hand and then typed it up when I got home. Secondly, I could keep in touch with friends through email without having to use hotel business centres. Thirdly, I could upload and sort my photos as I went, including re-naming them. This always took ages when I returned home, and so I could keep on top of them on a daily basis. Finally, I could check the news. I hadn't seen any English newspapers and there didn't seem to be any English news on the television, but I could quickly scan through it on the internet. Not in that hotel though, as the phone calls were £1 a minute, so I just logged on, sent the messages I'd written, picked up new emails and logged off as fast as possible. I suspected that when I reached Rio, everything would be a lot cheaper because there was more competition, so I'd be able to catch up with what had been happening in the world then.

Throughout all of this, I kept glancing out towards the Falls and I swear they got closer every time I looked at them.

I had a soak in the bath and then dressed for dinner. Not that I "dress" for dinner as shorts and a T-shirt would do. I needed to pack up that evening, as it was an early start in the morning when I would go straight from the hotel to the Brazilian side of the Falls and then to the airport for my flight. I went to collect my damp things from the balcony, but only my shorts and bra were dry. The vest and socks were still soaking, as were my trainers. The vest and socks were not a problem because I could wrap them in a towel in my suitcase and get them washed and cleaned in Rio. The trainers though were a big problem because I wanted to wear them the next day and it was highly unlikely that they would dry through for at least another twenty four hours, possibly longer. Oh dear, the shorts were in a mess, and I suddenly remembered that half way on the walk back up from the Falls I had sat down for a rest on brown soil. thinking my shorts were dry enough, but they now looked like I had suffered an unfortunate "accident". There would definitely be a few items going to the laundry in Rio.

I ate a la carte again, and added variety to my diet by consuming a bowl of delicious fish soup before following this with a steak, of course, which was much tastier than the one I had eaten the previous evening. I also insisted on ordering everything in Spanish as I'd never learn if I didn't use it. Unfortunately, as I hadn't done anything in Spanish for six months, I really had to search my brain cells for even a simple word, but the waiters were kind and patient and allowed me the time to compose even a small sentence.

I had a fantastic day and felt in great spirits. Iguazu Falls are a must for anyone travelling to South America, and although my legs were a little tired, it had definitely been worth doing all the trails.

Brazil here I come: December 19th

I was up, packed and checked out by 07:30 - ready and waiting for Ciro. It was fair to say that my shoulders were glowing somewhat that morning, so I'd worn a short sleeved T-shirt to keep them covered until they returned to a normal colour.

The agenda for the morning was to cross to the Brazilian side of the Falls, have a walk through their national park, which was much smaller than the Argentinean side, and then head to the airport for my 11:30 flight to Rio. As we drove to the national park, I was curious about the children I saw in the streets.

"Ciro, I'm interested about the school system here, because some children are dressed in school uniform, and clearly on their way to lessons, whilst others are playing in the street".

"Suzanne," he replied, "We have an unusual approach here in Brazil. If you do well in your school term tests and have been a good pupil, you are allowed to break up for Christmas holiday early, about the seventh or eighth of December. If, however, you have been naughty or your grades are not up to scratch, then you can't break up until about the 22nd or 23rd.That is why you see some children playing whilst other have to continue going to school."

"That must be one hell of an incentive for kids to work hard and behave at school." I quizzed.

"You would think so," Ciro sighed, "but some children are just naughty all of the time."

I'd paid Ciro the money for the tours, and was then somewhat surprised that I had to also pay the entrance fee to get into the park, about £8. Iguazu may be one of the most stunning places I will ever visit in my lifetime, but wow, it had been an expensive few days. Most of the payments had to be made in cash, so I was just a little concerned that my currency wouldn't last out the holiday. I would have to use my Visa card at every possible opportunity, not that there had been many so far.

If I had thought that the Argentinean side of the Falls was a photographer's paradise, then the Brazilian side must be Nirvana, with more rainbows than possible wishes you could ever come up with and some were so close that I really felt that if I reached out I'd be able to touch them.

Although there was a small walk to a platform, which was placed right next to a powerful fall, the main beauty of being on the Brazilian side was that you could take in the full panorama of the Falls. The day before I had been really close up, and although I'd seen the myriad of smaller falls, which I knew made up the bigger picture, it was still a breathless moment when I saw them linked up.

It was a shame that, in schools, I was taught a lot about the Niagara and Victoria Falls and yet had learned nothing of these dramatic and spectacular cascades, the noise of which boomed into your soul. The area was surrounded by dense jungle that suddenly opened up to display a massive crack in the earth's surface, caused by a volcanic eruption. I'd read that in the rainy season, the water can flow over the Falls at a rate of nearly half a million cubic feet per second. To put that in perspective, it is more water per second than an average family would use in a lifetime. It was like playing Monopoly. There were just too many noughts to really comprehend the size.

I could have stayed and watched the Falls changing colours and sparkling like Aladdin's cave for hours, but I had a flight to catch. It was with sadness that I pulled myself away from them, ensuring that I looked out of the window as we drove away to see the last little part of the Falls enveloped by the impenetrable jungle.

Foz do Iguaçu International Airport was not too busy, so the check-in was pretty speedy. With time to spare, I changed some money so that I had Brazilian Reals before I reached Rio, and then I sauntered through to departures. As I queued for the plane I was irritated by a couple of children messing about behind me, and three young girls, chewing gum loudly and popping it, who were obviously going off to Rio for a few days "fun". I hoped that I would be nowhere near the kids on the plane, so when I checked in I requested "an aisle seat please, nowhere near children."

A rather disturbing incident happened at the gate. We were all told that due to new legislation, we would have to complete the back of our boarding cards before we handed them in to board. They asked for your name, passport number and a next of kin's name and phone number. Considering how much travel I did for business, it was the first time that I had been asked for my next of kin details immediately before flying. Scary. Were they expecting to crash, to be shot down or blown up? Was there a code red in force?

Joe was effectively my next of kin. He was not only my best friend and surrogate brother, but also one of the executors of my will. However, I didn't know his phone number because I had him pre-programmed on both my mobile and home telephone .I had his details on my laptop but I wasn't about to get that out in the departure lounge, so I put down my father's name and number instead as it was the only phone number I knew by heart.

I found my seat on the plane, only to find that I had the two noisy, fidgety, bubblegum popping kids behind me. I thought I was having a back massage with all the pummelling that was going on. Perhaps the next of kin forms were required for throttled kids? Thankfully, the flight was just under two hours, and I was pleased when we touched down at Galeão–Antonio Carlos Jobim International Airport. I didn't think I'd ever been to an airport with such a long name. It had originally been named after the beach in front of the terminal, Galleon Beach in English, but then had its name extended by adding Antonio Carlos Jobim, the famous Latin jazz musician who wrote numbers such as The Girl from Ipanema, who had been born in Rio.

Getting my luggage was a bit of a wait, but on exiting the baggage claim area, I instantly spotted the "Susan Rogers" sign, and I introduced myself to Fatema. She was a slightly plump, well bronzed Latina with dyed hair that had been growing out for some months, aged somewhere between thirty and forty and looking exceptionally bored and irritated that she had to do a day's work. I didn't get a welcome as all she said was "this way madam" and pointed to one of the exits. The driver, who had been waiting by the exit to finish his cigarette, grunted a nod at me, then went off in search of his car. I had to carry my own luggage, but the suitcase had wheels, albeit slightly wobbly, so it was no big deal. Before we had even reached the car Fatema started her patter. She was clearly only going to impart the most important information so that she didn't waste too many words, and she regurgitated it all like a robot rather than a tour guide passionate about her city. She also quite evidently wanted to drop me off at the hotel and get on with the rest of her day as soon as possible. Needless to say, I didn't take to her.

I looked out of the car window en route to the hotel to see what I expected to be the stunning Corcovada, the lumpy mountain with the awesome Christ the Redeemer statue reigning over the city, and also Sugarloaf mountain, so named because of its shape, though, as I had never seen a sugarloaf, I had no idea how accurate a description this was. I found out later that it wasn't named after a loaf of bread, but rather, when the Portuguese were exporting sugar cane they piled it into moulds to facilitate loading it onto ships, and the conical shape of these moulds were called sugarloaves. The weather was overcast and although I spotted two world famous landmarks, they were not as imposing as I'd expected, so disappointment seeped in.

From the airport, we drove through the poorer southern area of the city, marked by the infamous favelas, or slums, a network of tightly packed crumbling buildings worming their way up the surrounding mountains, before entering a tunnel to get to the wealthier northern side. This may be the wealthier side of Rio, but the first adjective to spring to mind was grey. All the buildings seemed to be grey, and those tenement blocks with washing hanging from the windows exacerbated the greyness, rather than punctuate it with the bright vibrant colours that I'd associated with Rio before arriving.

Fatema started describing the tours available for me to book, then just pushed a leaflet into my hands so that I could read them for myself, as the exertion of just talking to me seemed to be too much effort for her.

"Madam, I tell you one thing," she droned, "Rio is a very dangerous place. We have a lot of poverty, a lot of drugs, a lot of thieving and murdering and a lot of guns. Many people are very poor and they see the rich peoples living by the beach and they see the tourists, and it is easy for them to steal and kill." Nice welcome I thought. There was a way of warning me to take my safety seriously and there was a way of making me feel like I had just arrived in the sewer of the world.

"If you go out of the hotel," she continued "leave everything in the safety box. I mean everything. Your watch, your purse, your jewellery and your camera. Just take a small amount of cash to get by whilst you are out, to buy a coffee or pay an entrance fee. If you have nice sunglasses, leave them in the hotel also. I have to collect you safely at the end of your stay, so I warn you seriously about these things. Be very careful when you go out of hotel and where you walk. You do not want to accidentally find yourself in a dangerous place. I think it would be good if you did an organised tour. Safer in a group. Crime rate very high and tourist is number

44

one target." With this she turned back to face the front and I could see that any conversation was over.

I looked at the brochure and selected a city tour that included Sugarloaf, Corcovada and a spectacular samba show with dinner

We drove along the beachfront and past the famous Palace Hotel on Copacabana beach. The driver automatically slowed down as he assumed that I would want a good look at it. Although it was an imposing building, it looked like it was ready for a wash-down, but most striking was the fact that at either side of it, and indeed as far as I could see up the side roads, the rest of the area was a combination of shabby grey concrete hotels or apartment buildings. Because of the glamour associated with the Copacabana Palace and its beach, I had imagined this area of the city to look glitzy and ridiculously opulent, like the casinos and hotels of Monte Carlo, but it just looked grey and sad.

The road arched around the scalloped Copacabana beach and then entered the next scallop of Ipanema beach. The front buildings were even more grey and sad, and it was clearly a second class area to Copacabana. We reached the Hotel Ipanema Plaza. I had expected a moderately glamorous place, judging by the brochure pictures I'd seen before booking, but in fact it was quite a grey and seedy three star hotel, and not even on the beachfront, but down a side road. So much for brochure accuracy.

Fatema handed over the vouchers for my trips that she had written out whilst I checked in, and said she would see me on the Wednesday morning at 09:00 to take me back to the airport.

Although the reception and corridors looked like they were screaming out for a refurbishment, I had great hopes for the room, as reception had told me that I'd been given a complimentary room upgrade. The room was definitely larger than an average hotel room, but it smelt mouldy and fusty. Luckily in Buenos Aires I'd bought a small packet of incense, and I burned three sticks to get rid of the smell. The room had air conditioning but no temperature control, so it was either on or off. I sorted out my suitcase as I hadn't unpacked since the start of the holiday. It wasn't worth it for a night here and a night there. However, I needed some washing done; I was travelling pretty light on the basis that I would be able to find laundry services at most of the hotels I was staying at, so I had a partial sort out and popped the dirty washing into the hotel bag provided.

I wanted to go out and explore. However, it was starting to get dark and I was actually quite frightened to go out. I'd seen too many documentaries on Rio, and these, backed up by Fatema's advice, made me fear for my safety. Instead I caught up with my diary, sent a few emails and hoped that I would survive Rio.

I ate in the hotel that evening, partly because I was too afraid to go out in the dark and partly because when I checked in I was given a 20% discount voucher for eating in the hotel. I ordered mussels for my starter, which were excellent, and surprise surprise, a steak for my main course, which again was decidedly average. What had happened to all the wonderful places I had eaten in during business trips to South America? I must have been taken to the best ones, as I had yet to have a steak that lived up to my expectations. Or perhaps my expectations were too high? I certainly missed South American beef when I returned to the UK, but perhaps I'd put it on a higher pedestal than it deserved.

I again reflected on eating alone, and it didn't bother me at all. Indeed, even back home, if I fancied eating out, I would just head out alone without even thinking to phone anyone to see if they wanted to come. I finished reading my second John Grisham easy-read holiday book, but it hadn't been that enjoyable. Not as absorbing as his previous books. I still had half the meal to go so I opened the next book, Angels and Demons. Having been totally unable to put down The Da Vinci Code a few weeks before the holiday, I had bought another couple of Dan Brown's books at the airport.

After dinner I fancied a cigarette, but didn't have any, so asked at reception where I could buy a packet. There wasn't a shop in the hotel but I was told I could get them at the bar. I sauntered through to the bar and asked the barman,

"Podría tener un paquete de cigarillos por favor?"

The barman produced a large bunch of keys and unlocked the cabinet behind the bar. Inside the cabinet was a box about the size of two shoeboxes, and he pulled this out and placed it on the counter. It had a padlock on it. He then fumbled in another drawer for a different bunch of keys and undid the padlock. Inside was a small selection of cigarettes and I pointed to the Marlboro. I wouldn't have thought that they needed that level of security actually inside the hotel, which made me think that Rio really must be a very scary place to visit.

Back in the room I listened to a Sparkies recording. I tried to record most of our band rehearsals so that we could listen and learn. I only had a small digital recorder and I would clip the mic to one of the branches of a large cheese plant. I had a sudden yearning to play my accordion, but I wouldn't see Sparky again for over two weeks. I had taken a small, plastic child's keyboard on my previous holiday to Vietnam (why??? – you need to read the book), but that had long since found its way into a bag of jumble.

I logged on to pick up my emails and Joe was online. After swapping a few instant messages I said, "bugger it, I'm going to give you a quick call." He wanted to know whether I was enjoying the holiday and how I was feeling. I said that I'd thoroughly enjoyed Iguazu, and that it was nothing short of magical, but my first impressions of Rio were not that favourable. He said he didn't mean the sights and places, but how I was feeling in myself. I replied that I had no problems on that front. I wasn't feeling lonely and was absolutely comfortable with my own company. I did tell him, however, that I'd made a load of wishes on the Iguazu rainbows, but I wasn't going to break the spell and tell him what they were.

Samba in Rio: December 20th

I was up bright and early, ready for my trip up Corcovado. Breakfast at this hotel was even more under whelming than at the previous venues. Perhaps breakfast just wasn't such a big deal in Brazil?

I was extremely conscious of the security warnings I'd been given, so I only took my camera, video camera and a small amount of money out with me. The cameras were buried deep at the bottom of my day bag. A car picked me up and took me to the bus that was waiting outside of the Copacabana Palace Hotel. As we cruised along the seafront, I thought again that, considering the location and the beautiful sandy beaches, it had to be the ugliest seafront that I had ever seen. Tall, grey, run-down buildings without a glimmer of the glamour that is so often associated with this city.

After joining the bus we crawled back along Copacabana, picking up tourists from the other hotels. We were joined at the last hotel by a guy with a huge video camera. He was introduced to us as the cameraman filming the day; at the end we would be able to buy a video or DVD from him which would consist of the "film of the day" plus other materials, such as Carnival in Rio. I was dangerously close to vomiting. I had no intention of purchasing a DVD, but I wasn't especially happy that I'd appear on film.

As the bus headed off to the first port of call, I prepared myself against thieves. I took off my watch and bum bag and pushed them to the bottom of my backpack, and then put my sarong over the top of them, if someone managed to unzip the bag and put their hand in it, by the time they reached the cameras and bum bag I'd have felt it. However, I didn't want the thieves to get that far, so I fastened the zip with a small suitcase padlock, and then, just to be on the safe side, I wrapped the backpack straps around my arms twice and held it close to my body.

We arrived at the base of Corcovada, the name of the mountain which means hunchback, and disembarked to take the cog train up to the top. We passed through jungle and the journey took about 20 minutes. It was a pretty steep ride and I had made the mistake of taking a seat that faces backwards, thinking that I could view the panorama as we ascended. All the way up, I felt that I was about to slip off the seat into the lap of the person facing me. It was remarkable that this unique railway, constructed over one hundred years ago, still ferried people up the steep sides of the mountain.

Despite what must have come across as despondency about Rio up to this point, I have to say that the statue of Christ the Redeemer (Cristo Redentor) at the top was extremely impressive, as were the views over the city. You couldn't tell how seedy it was 2,340ft up a mountain and looking down. Each time I took a camera out to take some photos, I wrapped the backpack round my foot just in case someone tried to half inch it. I was being either ultra cautious or extremely paranoid.

The statue, which was made of reinforced concrete and soapstone, stands nearly one hundred feet high, and the span of the outstretched arms are also nearly one hundred feet. It was made in France and transported in parts to be constructed, which took nine years, and it was finally completed in 1931.

Standing at the bottom of the plinth and looking up at the slightly bended face of Christ looking down, was truly an awesome feeling, even for an atheist. Not entirely surprising as the statue is one of the most iconic sights in the world, it was very crowded at the top, but it was a visit that I wouldn't have missed for the world.

The sky was a little overcast, but it wasn't cold, and thank goodness it wasn't too hazy to spoil the views.

Some people had come up in minibuses because the wait at the train station was too long, but for the experience, it would have to be the rickety old train every time. During the journey back down, a group of brightly dressed buskers with wide beaming smiles joined us and played some Samba. Now this was what Rio was about and I gladly delved into my pocket to throw some coins into the tambourine that was passed around just before we arrived back at the bottom of the mountain.

The tour was then supposed to include the beaches, however, we only stopped very briefly at Leblon beach, the longest of the beaches in Rio, and then just to be told that we were there, not even having the opportunity to get out of the coach. Within a few minutes I was turfed out at Ipanema beach, to walk back to my hotel. I only had to cross the seafront promenade and walk one hundred yards up a fairly wide side street to the hotel, but I was clutching my bag as if it contained gold bullion and was constantly looking around me. In the middle of the road I realised that nobody was around me and

I whipped out my camera to take a couple of shots, then stashed it away and almost ran back to the hotel.

Visiting Corcovado with the statue and views over Rio and the quaint old train was breathtaking, but the rest of the tour was pants. I felt like a sheep being herded around and the "guide", who never even introduced himself, was so poor that I did my own guiding from my handbook. Needless to say, he didn't get a tip.

Back at the hotel, I ventured up to the roof to see what sort of view I had. I could see several favelas built into the mountains so rickety and precipitously clinging to the hillside that it was a wonder that they didn't all collapse on themselves. Looking at them, I could understand why such huge swathes are wiped out when there is a landslide. I also had a good side view of Corcovado and the statue, though it was some way in the distance.

I desperately wanted to go out and explore, but was actually scared shitless of going out by myself. In the end however, I decided that I would leave everything in the hotel room: bum bag, watch and even my sunglasses. I'd take a little cash and go for a walk. I had 20 Reals in each pocket, about £10 in total. My sunglasses had prescription lenses, so I couldn't afford to risk having them stolen, and because of the bright glaring sun they were an essential accessory.

My guidebook indicated that the piano bar where Jobim wrote and first performed The Girl from Ipanema was just a few blocks from the hotel, so I set out in search of it. I covered several blocks, walking up and down each side street, but didn't find any piano bars at all, let alone the one I was looking for.

The locals must have thought that I had some sort of walking impediment. I was walking with both hands in my shorts pockets so that nobody could steal my cash, and I was weaving around as a skier does when traversing a slope. On top of this I was doing a constant 270 degree scan to check who was around me. I would have received a diploma from the Ministry of Silly Walks had they been there to watch me. However, I have to say that it didn't actually feel dangerous out, despite spying one or two dodgy looking characters. Perhaps the local tourist board was so worried about any bad press from tourists being attacked or robbed, that they beefed up the warnings to ensure that all antennae were primed. I wandered around some of the shops, and was surprised that they were not that cheap. It was all window shopping anyway, as I only had the 20 Reals with me, but I liked to get a feel for a culture by walking around their shopping areas. There are so many places these days where the big global brands have such a presence that frankly you could be in any city in the world once inside a shopping centre, but there would always be a few local shops that afforded interest. I noticed that in some of the clothing and footwear shops, items were not only marked up with their full price, but also how much it would cost to buy in instalments. So even though it was not cheap compared with England, and would appear even more expensive to the locals whose average salary was about a fifth of that in the UK, there were obviously ways and means to help them afford new clothes and footwear. In reality it was no different from people back home, buying from a catalogue and spreading the cost over a few months, it was just unusual to see it in a shop window.

I stopped at a little café to have a coffee and a piece of cake, sitting on a high stool with my arms down by my sides covering my pockets just in case.

After surviving about an hour of wandering around the area the sun came out, so, as I hadn't succeeded in finding the infamous piano bar, I decided to brave a walk along Ipanema beach towards Copacabana. It was only about a mile. I walked on the promenade not the actual beach, as I have an aversion to getting sand in every crevice, and although I felt pretty safe, it was somewhat disconcerting that, at what was effectively a beach resort, every fifty yards there was a policeman on patrol. Some just had truncheons, but many others were carrying guns and were wearing flak jackets. On the one hand, it made you feel safe with their presence. On the other hand, they wouldn't have so many police on patrol if they didn't have problems, so it was a double-edged sword. It was a real shame that I didn't have my camera with me because although the beach was largely empty: there were people surfing and there were some pretty views over to the little islands now that the sun was out. But it just wasn't worth the risk, even if a potential robber was mowed down with a hail of bullets by the police. I passed a sign showing the date and temperature. It was 40 degrees, the sun was beating down and I had a mile to walk back to the hotel.

In the room, I gave Joe a quick call to wish him happy Christmas, as he was heading off to his girlfriend's the next day and it would be the last chance I'd get to speak to him until after Christmas. He told me that it was extremely cold in England and that a white Christmas had been forecast.

My laundry has been returned, which was a relief as I was down to my last set of underwear, but I was not over jubilant as my white bras had come back biscuit coloured.

I got ready for my evening out. The pickup was supposed to be 19:15, but the coach didn't arrive until 19:45. The dinner was at a Churrascaria: a South American BBQ where you could eat as much as you want and they kept bringing different types of meat on skewers to the table. I had a disc like a round beer mat which was green on one side and meant "*please give me more food*" and red on the other, "*please stop feeding me*". There were only a couple of English speaking people on the coach, two girls who quite frankly looked like a pair of tarts, so I sat with an older Columbian couple, and between my limited Spanish and their limited English, we actually had an extremely pleasant dinner and a lot of laughs. My sign language, charades and pointing at things helped out a lot, as their limited English was significantly more than my limited Spanish. The meat just kept on coming. Beef, lamb, pork, chicken and local sausages in every possible cut: rump, sirloin, fillet and so on and it was utterly delicious. I must have eaten the equivalent of half a cow by the time it was ready to leave for the show.

The show was a wonderful spectacle the likes of which I had never seen before. The commentator said that we would see different dances from across different periods of Brazilian history. The music went straight to your soul and the costumes were out of this world. How the dancers were able to wear them and move

55

would always remain a miracle to me. Many had brightly coloured crinoline dresses with a huge matching circle of colour attached to their backs so that they looked like giant butterflies. Some were themed, such as the lady with music notes printed around the hem of her voluminous skirt and a keyboard motif circling the dials attached to her back. The amount of colour and vibrancy I saw in an hour and a half, more than made up for the grey buildings festooning Rio.

I found the drummers especially fascinating, because during a Jazz Summer School that I had attended earlier in the year, there had been a half a day tutorial about the specific Samba rhythm, and not only the roles of the different drums but indeed anything that made a sound; rattles, bits of metal, slices of wood and so on. Every percussionist in a Samba band has an individual role to play and has a distinct beat and rhythm. To the untrained ear it was just bloody good drumming, but after the Summer School training, I watched and listened to each of them individually, and sure enough, they were following the "rules". It was a huge pleasure to see the theory in action.

During the show, I sat next to an American chap from Los Angeles and we chatted amiably about our respective holidays. He was also travelling alone and was doing virtually the same itinerary as me but the other way round, so that his next port of call was Iguazu. He seemed like a really decent chap with many interests the same as my own, but at the end of the show we wished each other a pleasant holiday and went our separate ways. It was one of those moments where it fleetingly crossed my mind "in another time in another place…"

Joe frequently asked me if I suffered loneliness, but despite having lonely pangs in the past, the answer was about 99% no. If I feel like a lonely moment is about to hit, I switch into "fantasy mode". I have little clips of make believe stories in my head and heart, which I just play to myself and the moment passes. Sometimes, the power of feeling associated with these is so strong it almost feels real. We all have our own individual coping mechanisms and this is one of mine. Another coping mechanism is to re-read recent emails, like, for example, one from Joe commenting on how much courage he thought I had to face a three week holiday alone. This would not have been the case if I hadn't experienced travelling alone when I visited Vietnam last year. I didn't plan to be alone at that time, but had no choice in the matter. I thoroughly enjoyed it though, and I'm so glad I've done it alone again. In fact, during the trip tour to Corcovada, I really resented being in a group, even though it was only for half a day. However, as Rio was not a place to sightsee by myself and the individual tour guides were too expensive, I was stuck between the infamous rock and a hard place, and for the sake of seeing the few main sights the only option was to join the organised tour.

My other coping mechanism is to remember that I am a cockroach.

Years earlier, I was working at Kraft Foods and we were on an outward-bound team-building course. In the evening the trainers would "play" management games with us. One of them was to describe the people in our team as animals. It was Mike's turn, a brand manager who I didn't think knew me that well.

"I think Fiona is a gazelle" he said.

"Interesting" said the trainer in a tone that said that he come across lots of gazelles before, "and why is that?"

"Well," continued Mike, "she is thin and lithe and darts around the office all the time."

"And Ivor?" prompted the trainer.

"Ivor would definitely be a bear because on the surface he appears to be big and gruff, but actually he's a little softie on the inside."

"And Susan?"

"Susan would be a cockroach." There was stunned silence.

"Thanks Mike," I chipped in, "I've always wanted to be called a cockroach! Whenever I have come across one, I just stamp on it." The trainer sat up and listened intently at this point, because he had never had anyone being described as a cockroach before during his training sessions.

"I saw a programme on television a few weeks ago," said Mike. "It was about the potential devastation if there were to be a nuclear war. The theorists say that the only creature that would survive would be the cockroach." Mike paused for effect then concluded, "My perception of Susan is that whatever life throws at her, she survives. She brushes herself down and bounces back. She is an example of a true survivor." So when I hit wobbly moments in my life, I remember that I'm a cockroach and the moment passes quickly. The problem though with being a cockroach is that people can see you as being stronger than you are, and forget that cockroaches probably have feelings too. I doubt that Mike, wherever he is now, remembers that training course, but he had an insight into me that I hadn't, and one that still lasts and is powerful. Thank you Mike.

Back in my hotel room, my legs started to itch and I noticed that I'd been bitten several times, probably in the theatre during the show. As they were around my ankles I doubted they were mosquitoes and indeed were most likely to be fleas. I rubbed some anti-histamine cream on them, and then downloaded the photos from the evening.

It was quite late, but I didn't have to rush to get up the next day as my tour of Sugarloaf and the City wasn't until the afternoon.

Sugarloaf: December 21st

I had a leisurely start to the day as the tour was not until 14:15, it was dark and thundery outside so I had no desire to go out. I picked up and responded to emails, caught up with my diary and started sorting through the photos I'd already taken. Not for the first time, I was thankful for the invention of digital cameras, because if I had taken this many snaps with film, I'd have had to take out a second mortgage on return to pay for the developing.

Preparing to go down for breakfast was a major undertaking because I wanted to lock everything away before I left the room. Part of it was "self inflicted" because it was my choice to take my laptop, it's associated cables, a memory stick and so on, not to mention my passport, money and travellers cheques, but I just didn't want to leave anything lying around in case it went walkies.

Memory sticks were quite new at the time and therefore expensive, but at about half the size of a cigarette lighter it was no problem to take it with me as I planned to download photographs as I went, so that I'd have a back up if anything happened to the laptop such as humidity or light fingers.

Returning to my room after breakfast, I settled down to transfer the photos, but I just couldn't find the memory stick. I'd last seen it on the desk, but was certain that I'd locked it in the safe before breakfast, but it was in neither of these place. I emptied out the hotel safe, and all the possible "hiding places" in my suitcase; after about twenty minutes of looking, I was convinced that I must have left it out and it had gone walkies. But no, it turned up in the fold of my

61

passport holder, which had been in the safe, and the panic was over.

Looking out of the window I saw the rain pouring down and the clouds descending, reducing the prospect of seeing anything that afternoon from Sugarloaf.

I decided to have a light lunch before the tour to prevent me getting the munchies whilst I was out, and having enjoyed the mussels so much a couple of nights previously, I ordered them again. Initially I thought about eating outside as there was a raised, covered area, like a little patio, however, the stench of the drains after the rain was overpoweringly pungent, so I chose a table inside. Whilst I was waiting for my food I caught generous whiffs of sewer, and noticed that the patio windows to the street had been opened. I gesticulated to the waitress to close them, shrivelling up my face and holding my nose to get the message across. She closed them, but a woman sitting nearby with a baby got up and opened them again. I could see the waitress explaining to her that I wanted them closed because of the smell, yet the woman clearly wanted them open for her baby to have "fresh air". I didn't want to get into an argument, so I gesticulated that I'd go and sit in the back part of the restaurant, which clearly didn't please the staff as they didn't usually use that part of the dining room at lunchtime. To almost confirm that it just wasn't my day, I managed to splash greasy mussel liquor down the front of my vest. It was my favourite, a deep fuchsia pink vest with a square neck line. Now that my tan had progressed from red to brown, I had hoped that one of the other tourists would take a photo of me, but then I wasn't so sure I'd want permanent evidence of my sloppy misfortune.

The tour, like the others, was unsurprisingly late in starting, and was described as a city tour followed by an ascent up Sugarloaf.

Within minutes I wondered why anyone would possibly want to see this city as it offered virtually nothing of interest. There were only ten of us on a fifty-seater coach, and the first stop was the Maracana football stadium. The only two men on the coach leapt off to take pictures, snapping the stadium from as many angles as they could, and then swapping cameras so that they would each have a photograph of themselves outside this revered football building. From Corcovado it had looked like a giant flying saucer that had landed in the centre of Rio, yet down on the ground it was yet another grey concrete building. I remained on the coach. I couldn't understand why we had stopped there - it wasn't even listed in the guide books as worth seeing. I overheard the conversation between the two men as they returned to the coach.

"Did you see that sign over there, you can get guided tours of the stadium."

"Really?"

"Yes. I wonder if they are open tomorrow?"

The streets lacked character and were dirty. Just row upon row of grimy grey concrete. The next stop was the new Catholic cathedral, called Catedral Metropolitana de São Sebastião do Rio de Janeiro. Inside it was an interestingly shaped conical building with impressive stained glass windows, but from the outside, it was nothing more than shabby concrete blocks, arranged in a pyramid with waffle-effect sides, resembling an upside down tea strainer. I couldn't get a decent photo of the stained glass windows because it was too dark inside so I bought a postcard. Whilst looking at the selection I noticed that those featuring the outside of the church made it look like a stunning modern, clean and bright structure, so I bought an outside postcard as well to contrast it with the photo I'd just taken of the building with broken windows and walls that were well past a needed cleanup . I then examined the other general postcards and pictures for sale. All of them showed a clean, bright, vibrant city with atmosphere and I wondered if I was in the same place. I concluded that all of the postcards must either be from photos taken 20 years ago, or severely airbrushed. Rio was the pits, and none of the postcards gave a genuine flavour of the place.

After the church, we piled back on the coach. Considering that there were five places for each person, a guy, who was moving around the coach constantly to get photos from every angle and who clearly had his video camera glued to his hand, sat in front of me for a rest from photography and then tipped his seat right back so that he was almost on my knees. The same guy had done this to me during the tour the day before, but this time he got a knee in his back and he sharply returned his seat back to its upright position. I loathed "tour groups" and if it wasn't for the fact that I really felt uncomfortable in this city, I'd have gone out and organised my own tours.

The final stop before Sugarloaf was the open stadium area where the carnival parades start during the season, and where they held the carnival dancing shows. Again, it was in hideous dirty concrete and looked like a building site even though there was no obvious construction within sight. I was starting to suspect that the only time Rio comes alive, vibrant and colourful, is during Carnival, but I won't be back to see it and this would be my one and only visit to this grey metropolis. What surprised me most was that what looked like a colourful street in all the carnival photos and movies you see, is actually nothing more than a concrete corridor a few hundred metres long with tiered seating up both sides.

We then made our way to the cable car for the trip up Sugarloaf mountain. It was completed in two stages, and it was raining quite hard by the time we started our ascent. Towards the top, we disappeared completely into cloud, so the view of Rio was absolutely zero. It was a good job that I'd had a reasonable view the previous day from Corcovada, however it would have been nice to see the reverse. We seemed to be rushed fairly quickly back to the cable car for the descent, but this was no great disappointment as we hadn't been able to see anything at all, and the rain was plainly set in for the rest of the day.

I had observed the local people today during the trip and there didn't appear to be such a thing as a "Brazilian looking person", presumably because of the influx of different people over the years. Some looked like they could be British, others southern European with a slightly Latin look, some looked a little oriental, and others looked almost black African. Many of the women seemed to be stunningly beautiful from a distance, but when I got closer, they were wearing heavy makeup trowelled over pot-marked faces, large pouting lips and angry eyes. The men seemed to scowl a lot, and weren't a patch on their handsome Argentinean neighbours. There was also an unfortunately high proportion of the men snorting phlegm left right and centre, and I noticed when we stopped at one set of traffic lights just how many were fiddling with their private bits. There could be a huge marketing opportunity here to introduce comfortable underwear.

Returning to the hotel after a decidedly unadventurous afternoon out, I packed everything up ready to leave the next morning.

I picked up some emails, one of which was from a friend suggesting that I changed the name of my house to Rogers International so that my business stationery looked as if it was based in a large office. However, I already had that one sussed as the address was going to be First floor, X House, Aylesbury, and indeed it worked as many people thought that X house was a modern purpose built office block and that I occupied the whole first floor. In fact, it was actually my spare bedroom which truthfully was on the first floor.

I ate in the hotel again as I didn't want to venture out. The menu wasn't especially inspiring, so I opted for a burger and fries. Yes, I know, hardly traditional Brazilian food, but I'd seen one served on the next table and had to admit that the burger looked handmade and juicy.

Irony of ironies, I was reading Dan Brown's Deception Point whilst I ate, and came across the following paragraph:

"It was not so much the bugs abundance that impressed as it was their resilience. From the Antarctic ice beetle to Death Valley sun scorpion, bugs happily inhabited deadly ranges in temperature, dryness and even pressure. They had also mastered exposure to the most deadly force known in the universe – radiation. Following a nuclear test in 1945, air force officers had donned radiation suits and examined ground zero only to discover cockroaches and ants happily carrying on as if nothing had happened.

Wow, it was the first time I'd come across corroborating evidence for Mike from Kraft Foods theory.

Natal: December 22nd

I had a bad night's sleep, however, I awoke positive and looking forward to the day ahead. Yippee I was moving on and escaping from Rio. I was up, dressed, packed and ready by 07:00 even though my pick up wasn't until 09:00.

After a light breakfast, I sat and read in the lobby whilst waiting for Fatema, hoping that on this occasion she would be on time and everything would run to plan. She arrived only a few minutes late wearing the same scowling face of boredom as when I'd first met her.

The airport was a little bit of a pain with a long queue for check in, but again, I didn't really care as I was heading in the right direction. Away from Rio. My luggage was decreasing in weight. It had started at twenty one kilos and was now down to nineteen as I discarded books, and other things en route. This was, of course, before the introduction of Kindle and tablets where you can take a whole library with you for a few grams, so for a three weeks trip I was certain that half the weight was paperbacks. I also had the idea that, towards the end of the holiday when I'd lightened my load by leaving holiday books around South America, I'd have room for some local goodies to bring back, without going through UK customs looking overly burdened. So far though, I hadn't seen anything that I desperately wanted to bring back as a souvenir. There were quite a lot of wooden carved "things", but as my house seemed to be already overflowing with such trinkets, I had decided that I would only get something that I fell in love with and not just an item that instantly caught my eye.

At least it was going to be easy on gifts for friends back home. They would all get some Brazilian coffee beans, except for Joe, who doesn't drink much coffee. He'd asked me to get him a memory stick from duty free, so I'd give him that as a gift. It seems crazy now that one would wait to get to duty free to get a memory stick, when they are almost given away in cereal packets these days.

I would no doubt get something for myself to remind me of the holiday, but at the moment I hadn't seen anything. I suspected that it may be a coat or jacket as I hadn't taken one with me because of the heat. However, I knew that when I got to Patagonia, if it was as cold as I expected it to be, I'd buy one there. No point in carrying a heavy coat for two and a half weeks in sweltering heat.

The flight was a nightmare and even dented my ebullient mood for the duration. There was a five or six-year-old girl sitting directly in front of me, and she spent the entire three hours screaming, squealing, fidgeting, standing up and poking over the chair. I almost committed murder. Her parents were completely oblivious to the noise and commotion she was causing, despite thundery looks from other passengers, in addition to myself.

The plane arrived in Natal on the North east coast of Brazil, and my guide, Junior, was waiting for me. He obviously used his own car, rather than have a driver, and we piled into his little runabout. As we drove to the hotel, my first impressions of Natal was that it was just being constructed as there was much building work going

70

on, but it was all relatively low rise. I was staying just out of the main town of Ponta Negro and Junior told me that it was out of the tourist area, which suited me just fine.

We arrived at the hotel Manary Praia, and it was absolutely delightful. It reminded me of the pensions that you find in southern Turkey. There were probably no more than thirty rooms and the place had a warm family feeling about it. It had a commanding view over the Atlantic ocean, and the outside of the building had a hacienda feel with it's freshly painted walls in ochre and sandy pink and palm trees peppered around the grounds. There was a spacious swimming pool and a roof terrace restaurant. I literally felt the stresses of Rio slither away.

After checking in and gladly consuming the complimentary glass of mouth-watering freshly squeezed chilled exotic juices, Junior told me about the tours available. I'd already established that there was bugger all to see in the town, so definitely didn't want a "city tour" and, in any case, the place was so tranquil and serene that I had no qualms about wandering around by myself. The only two jaunts that appealed were a musical show (featuring accordions) together with dinner, and a half-day beach buggy trip into the sand dunes. However, the prices were horrendous, so I told him that I wasn't going to do any trips because they were too expensive, and thought that I could sort out dinner and a show by myself without any mark-up.

"There are options Suzanne" Junior explained, "These trips are through the official agency, and I know they add big mark up. I have friends and contacts that can do the trips for a much better price."

71

"How much?" I queried.

He took out a small calculator and started pressing buttons furiously, although I suspected that he already had the answer in his head before any results bleeped on the display. He then tilted his head on one side and slightly furrowed his brows as if the answer on the little machine was alarming, then looked up at me and smiled,

"I can do it all for two thirds of the price and I will give you a free taxi to the show."

It was now in the "slightly expensive" range rather than the "extortionate" range, so I smiled and agreed.

"Great!" he grinned, "You will get exactly the same tours but without the agency add-on rates."

He bade me farewell with,

"Enjoy your visit to this beautiful part of Brazil, and although you are very safe in the streets during the day, I suggest that you don't go out alone after 22.00." I nodded, shook his hand and headed to my room. I was finding Brazil a pretty expensive place to visit and it surprised me considering the large areas of poverty. I would have thought that they could attract a lot more tourism if the prices were better and bring greater income into the country. No wonder that so many British headed to Asia for winter sun rather than South America. The difference between the two continents was quite marked in this respect. In Asia, there was much more obvious and evident poverty, with persistent beggars and touts in your face, yet

I'd always felt safe in the various countries I'd visited. In Brazil, it was much less in your face and if you said "no" to a street seller they moved on to someone else. The poor areas were almost cities within cities that you saw from a distance but not close up, yet there was an air of needing to be cautious and alert wherever you went.

My room was just unquestionably lovely. Wooden fittings, tiled floor, a huge bigger than king size four-poster bed, and a balcony where I could sit and gaze out to sea. I'd been given a quiet room, which I had requested when I booked the holiday for all my hotels and this one was perfect. I'd allocated this part of the holiday for "rest and relaxation" for a few days, and I was delighted that it was so idyllic. The skies were bright Tuscan blue and the temperature was over forty degrees, yet the light breeze coming in from the sea didn't make it feel as blistering as it actually was.

As it was around mid afternoon, and I needed to change some cash, I walked to the nearest little shopping centre. It was only about 2 miles away and the first part was up a 45-degree slope to get to the road.

I found the shopping centre, which was modern but small, and then located the exchange place. I went to walk in, but a lady in front of me stopped me and politely told me to wait my turn. I didn't actually understand what she was saying, but she pointed to a notice and I got the message. Only one person at a time was allowed in the little unit. After about a twenty-minute wait, it was my turn, so I took out my traveller's cheques only to be told that they only exchange cash or Amex cheques. Blast! I'd only brought travellers cheques out with me and mine were Thomas Cook. He told me the bank down the road would change the cheque, so I walked another half a mile along a dusty road, only to find that it had closed five minutes previously. Double blast!

I should point out that when I say "he said" or "I said" that is not entirely true. English there was extremely limited, and my Portuguese was zero. It was not uncommon to find people in South America using Portunol, a blend of Spanish and Portuguese, so despite my lack of Portuguese, with a few Spanish words, and heaps of gesticulation, I managed to have what could loosely be called a "conversation". There was a little market just outside of the shopping centre, and I had a wander around just to take in the ambience, with no intention of buying anything. I noticed that the people here were more relaxed, friendly and smiley than they were in Rio and not especially in a hurry to get anywhere. It was as if I was in a different time zone where the pace of life had suddenly halved. I stopped and "chatted" to a couple of people who stopped me and asked which country I was from, and although it was difficult to hold a conversation, it clearly pleased them that I made an attempt to speak Spanish, which was closer to their language than English.

Back at the hotel I picked up my e-mails. A friend George had said that if I was in one place for long enough to send him the phone number he'd give me a call. I sent him the number for that hotel, but said that I thought he'd be crazy to call Brazil because of the cost. Half an hour later he gave me a call and although I still thought he was crazy, it was soothing to hear a friendly voice.

I had dinner, which was out on the patio around the pool and which was nothing short of excellent. Shrimps in garlic then steak with salad. I was brought a selection of oils and vinegars and the like for the salad. There was one very interesting one, a conical bottle stuffed with herbs, peppers and garlic. I drizzled some of that over the salad. On first tasting, I nearly went through the roof as it had the fire of molten lava. I demolished my first accompanying beer very quickly. However, the meal was first rate, the waiters very relaxed and pleasant and it was a great evening. I was slightly amused by having my beer served from a champagne bucket full of ice. Whilst I was halfway through the first beer, the waiter brought two more and placed them in the ice and gave me a cheeky look as if to say – they are ready for you if you want them. Nice touch. One of the pleasurable things about travelling alone is that you generally get friendly attentive service in restaurants. There was nothing "come on" about it, but as I was a bit of an oddity to the locals as a solo female traveller, it was almost like the waiters took me under their respective wings, and wanted to look after me. Quite cute really.

Money changing: December 23rd

I had a fantastic night's sleep and leapt out of bed full of energy and raring to go. I had escaped Rio and was now cocooned in the relative tranquillity of Natal.

I dived into the shower with gusto, wanting to be out and about exploring, and then realised that I needed to run a razor up my legs. When travelling, I didn't take my usual "lady razor" but standard Bic disposables. Also, I am actually more of a bath person than a shower person, the point being that I was using an unfamiliar razor standing up rather than lying down. It glided up my leg, not just taking the top layer of hair, but also a three inch sliver of skin just above my ankle. It wasn't that deep a cut, and it stung rather than hurt, but there was blood everywhere. Exiting the shower rapidly to dress the cut and taking extra special care with the slippery tiles, I managed to avoid the white floor towel yet still left a trail of blood behind me. Eventually it stopped bleeding and I cleaned up the mess. Not the best of starts to the day, but I was in such great spirits, nothing was going to dampen my adventure.

The plan of action was to leave the hotel at 08:30, walk down to the bank ready for their 09:00 opening, cash some travellers cheques, stop off at the exchange kiosk on the way back and change some sterling, and be back to the hotel before they finished serving breakfast at 10:00. What followed was a saga of "how to take four hours over changing money".

I arrived at the bank at 08:55 and joined the queue. It looked pretty long, about twenty people, but at least I was there early and it appeared to be large enough to have several cashiers. You had to go through a metal detector door before entering and it shut just as I approached it. I passed my bum bag through a little window and collected it on the other side. It was a very new, spacious bank, with lots of different booths, each with signs above them, and plenty of seating for whilst you wait your turn. I found the one marked Cambio, and as someone was already there, I waited. It was only at this point that I saw the sign saying that the Cambio opened at 10:15 (and they don't change five hundred Euro notes). Thankfully I didn't have any five hundred Euro notes, however, the opening time was a real pain. I decided to wait to speak to someone, just to check that they did indeed change traveller's cheques, and yes they did. I was given a number in the same manner as they do in a supermarket deli and my turn was number six ..... but still after 10:15.

I wasn't very happy, as this instantly meant that I was going to miss breakfast at the hotel, but I chose that rather than waste the time, I'd go to the shopping centre and change the cash, and then I could go back to the bank for 10:15 for the traveller's cheques. The Cambio kiosk was closed. I asked one of the shopping centre guards what time it opened and he pointed to the clock and then held up ten fingers. 10:00. It still wasn't worth going all the way back to the hotel just to come out again so I bought a bottle of water and sat outside the shopping centre waiting for the Cambio Kiosk to open, indulging in people watching as the town slowly came alive. At 09:55 I headed back inside, with plan bravo being to change the cash there, go back to the bank to change the traveller's cheques and be back at the hotel for around 10:30. There was already a

78

queue at the kiosk. I was number five. It opened and the first person sauntered in. He was in there for twenty minutes, and I had thought it was just a bureau de change place, yet clearly it offered cashing facilities for local cheques. Meanwhile the queue had grown outside, and some people were getting fractious and tapping on the glass window. In the queue in front of me was a Brazilian lady with her English husband. I chatted a little to them as they were interested in my holiday itinerary. After twenty minutes, the money changer came out and explained something to the restless crowd. It was clearly not good news, as the Brazilian lady confirmed.

"It is the computer. It is down. Not working today. He says there will be no more money changed this morning. Perhaps not even this afternoon." She shrugged, yet it was evident by her face and posture that this was not a surprise to her and quite clearly a regular occurrence.

I would have to scrub changing the cash, and just depend on the travellers cheques, so I stomped off back to the bank.

You may wonder why I spent so much time changing money, well it's because I've always travelled on the premise that I'll change a little here and there, partly because I don't want to carry loads of money with me, but also I don't want to get to the end of a holiday with a wad of foreign money that I can't change back in the UK. That morning I'd made the decision to change $200 of traveller's cheques and £100 sterling, as money changing was clearly more difficult here than anywhere else I'd experienced; and with Christmas rapidly approaching, I didn't want to get stuck again. The other problem was that I couldn't use the hole in walls to get my money, because after being mugged in Budapest. I'd had to cancel and re-order new cards, which, inconveniently due to the Christmas postal rush, hadn't arrived before I left England. I had a credit card with me, but didn't want to use it to get cash because of the low exchange rates combined with high card charges.

Back at the bank, the girl from earlier recognised me and pointed to a seat. I noticed that the person who was currently changing money was number nine. Through pigeon Spanish and gesticulation and waving my number around I told the girl that I must be next. At this point, a young, rough looking, Brazilian couple next to me start screeching that they were next and had been waiting and that I should go to the back of the queue. In my basic Spanish I explained that I was there at 09:00 and that I have ticket number six. By this time I was thirsty, dehydrated and dying for a toilet. The person currently at the counter took twenty five minutes to have her money changed and then the rough Brazilian couple jumped up and took her seat before I could. I waved my arms in despair at the female cashier who I first saw three hours ago and pointed to my watch. Thankfully the Brazilian couple were only seated for five minutes and soon as I saw them starting to raise their bums from the chair – I was in! This was much to the disgruntlement of another lady, but I was not moving. My bottom was on the seat and I WAS GOING TO GET MY MONEY CHANGED!

Even though I was now seated in the chair at the cashier's desk, she beckoned over the other lady and dealt with her first. Although I think her transaction would have taken ages anyway, I was sure that she slowed down to eek it out an additional ten minutes. Then eventually it was my turn. The girl asked if I spoke Portuguese and I said no. Her English was very basic. She pointed to the exchange rate, which was pretty awful at only 2.6 Reals to the dollar (I was getting three in Rio) and the line that said that each transaction cost $20. TWENTY US DOLLARS! However, I was stuck between a rock and a hard place, so I just told her to cash them. She had to take a photocopy of my passport, phone Thomas Cook for authentication of my cheques, and fill in a detailed computer screen. Just as she was about to press "go", a message flashed on the screen that the exchange rate has just changed. She smiled at me and said that she would have to start again. The transaction took twenty minutes. Once all the paperwork had been completed, I then had to take a slip of paper and join another queue to get my cash. By this time I'd lost track of the time, but I must have been in the second queue for another half hour. They had a rule in that bank that if you are an old person, a person with a baby, or ill / infirm, you could go straight to the front of the queue. Never had I been in a queue where I advanced backwards rather than forwards and pondered whether it would be worth wearing a bandage or an arm sling next time I had to change money.

Eventually I got my hands on my money and the cashier confirmed that they wouldn't change cash there, so I headed back to the hotel. I had to pass the shopping centre again and the Cambio Kiosk, and it seemed to be working again, and there was only one person inside. I waited for just five minutes and then it was my turn and they changed my cash, quickly and efficiently. Phew, mission accomplished. However, breakfast was a distant memory and it was now time for lunch. I stopped off at a little supermarket and bought a couple of beers before returning to the hotel around 13:00. The friendly chap on reception smiled at me. I knew he spoke English, so I said,

"I guess I've missed breakfast?" He replied with a grin.

"And lunch also, I think!"

I lay on the balcony of my room for a couple of hours, demolishing the remainder of the cashews I'd bought previously and three cans of beer. This was supposed to be the R&R part of the holiday, but I felt a little restless and needed a walk, so I ventured outside the hotel again. Whereas some people can go on holiday and then lie by a pool or stretch out on a beach for hour after hour, day after day, a few hours is about as much as I can manage, not because of the heat, but because I'm always itching to be "doing" something.

The hotel was built on a steep slope, so I had to go down several flights of stairs to get to the pool area, and then down some more steps and through a locked door to get to the beach promenade.

It was an exceptionally pleasant walk about a mile outside of the town. There were quite a lot of people on the beach and numerous entrepreneurs selling jewellery, towels and sarongs, but I wasn't pestered. When I reached the town I was a little peckish as I hadn't had breakfast or lunch and just a few handfuls of cashews and three small cans of beer, so I stopped off at a sidewalk café for a diet coke and a pizza. I chose a seafood pizza and it was one of the best I had ever eaten. Very thin crispy base, with oodles of topping; garlicky tomato and cheese with lots of fish and shrimps. I then headed back to the hotel to catch up with diary and prepare for my evening out.

I had an hour or so to kill before going out, so I just sat on my balcony and considered the holiday so far. Ok, so I had hated Rio, but at least I'd experienced it, and that was what holidays are for me – experiences, and I had really enjoyed everything else. I could even smile about the money exchange that morning. Frustrating, yes, but certainly an experience. I definitely preferred travelling alone than being in a tour group, and as long as I could keep in touch with my friends electronically, I didn't feel isolated. Indeed I was enjoying my own company more and more and wondered whether I had hermit tendencies.

I showered and changed for the evening out. A churrasceria dinner followed by a musical show, and I was hoping for accordions. Junior picked me up at 20:00 and I expected the format to be similar to Rio, insofar as he would drop me off at the restaurant, leave me to have my dinner and then take me to the show. I had my next book with me, Martin Amis' "Money", to read whilst slowly savouring what must be my favourite food type. It is effectively a barbecue. The passadores or meat waiters come to your table with skewers of meat and a knife. They explain what type and cut of meat it is and then you decide whether you want any. They will then either carve a slice, if it is a large piece of meat, or slip a piece off the skewer, if it is a smaller cut, or sausage or chicken wing, for example. There is emphasis on beef cuts, which suits me down to the ground. Different restaurants have different ways of serving you. In some, the waiter simply approaches you and asks if you want to try whatever he has on his skewer. In others there are non verbal signals to the waiter, for example, a round disc about the size of a beer mat that is green on one side and red on the other. If you display the green side it means "more meat please" and the red side means "not at the moment". Usually Churrascerias have a large salad bar that you can frequent as much as you like.

Junior however ate with me and he took me to a little churrasceria outside town.

"Suzanne, I take you to a very good churrasceria." He rolled his R's and I could almost feel the beef melting in my mouth. "It is a place that locals go to eat. It is not really a tourist restaurant, so you will be eating with locals", he added.

The food was excellent, and certainly the best meal of the holiday so far. The barbecue where they were cooking the meat was open into the restaurant, and as there were not many people eating, the chef beckoned me over so that he could show me how they cooked the food. He slotted meat onto the skewers, which were pointy at one end and hooked at the other, and then he hooked the skewers over the wood fire to cook the meat.

Whilst we were eating, Junior told me about his Dutch girlfriend who was staying with him over the Christmas period. He had met her when she was a tourist, they had hit it off instantly and had been seeing each other for about six months. He'd been over to see her in Holland once and she was back in Brazil for two months.

"Do you think you'll get married?" I asked inquisitively, and a sheepish grin spread across his face.

"Suzanne, we were very happy living together. Neither of us is especially religious and so I guess we thought we'd just carry on living together. But now she is pregnant. It wasn't planned, but equally we both knew that we were taking risks." Just as I thought he sounded like he was regretting the relationship as fate had played a hand, he grinned from ear to ear.

"I am thirty five years old and my girlfriend is thirty two years. I think if it hadn't happened by accident then we may have left it too late. So I now think that it is perhaps a good thing. However, I have a problem. She wants me to tell my mother, but I need time to get used to the idea. We only found out for definite yesterday when we had the pregnancy test done."

"Congratulations," I said, not sure what else to say. I could hardly say "I dislike children myself, so many commiserations".

"You are the first person I have told" he added shyly. "I am worried about what my mother will say. She is very religious and she doesn't like that we live together. But she is not a fanatical, and I think she will like the idea once she gets used to it. I don't want to tell her until after Christmas. We have all my relatives coming to stay. My uncles, my cousins, my cousins' partners and some children. It will be a big family gathering and she's been busy baking and cooking for the last week ready for all the family to descend tomorrow night. I think she is already under enough stress with the big cooking responsibility, so I will wait until it's all over."

After a couple of the meats had been served, Junior told me that he was going to teach me some Portuguese. Every time I said thank you, I said "gracias". He explained that although the waiters understood me, the correct way to say thank you is "obrigada" or obrigado if you are male.

Absolutely full to overflowing with delicious Brazilian beef, it was time for the show and I virtually staggered to my seat. We sat a little way from the front on a raised section to get a good view. It was quite a pleasant show demonstrating different dances from the region and very colourful, but wasn't as professional as the Samba show I'd seen in Rio, and yes, there was an accordionist, but only one and very much playing the background music with the rest of the band. Towards the end, the dancers came off the stage and pulled people up from the audience to join them. Junior asked if I wanted to get up and have a go.

"You must be joking," I laughed, "that sort of stuff is for the tourists!"

After the show, we headed back to the hotel and he told me that I would be picked up at 09:00 for the sand dune buggy trip and that one of his friends would be taking me. He then added,

"I may or may not see you for the airport run which is at 04:00 Monday morning. It depends what the agency says. They know that I have my girlfriend staying over Christmas and they do not want to burden me too much." So I wished him all the best, in case I didn't see him again. All in all, it was an extremely pleasant evening out with a "local".

As an afterthought, as if he should have been giving me historical or geographical information to enhance my visit, he suddenly told me that coffee is still the biggest export from Brazil, however, only the beans because the Brazilians can't make decent coffee. I was surprised, and he burst out laughing saying that Nescafe make better coffee. Brazilians just provide the beans. I reckoned that I'd only buy beans then for friends as holiday gifts.

I read a little before going to sleep, and I was just about to go to bed when I saw a lizard on my bed covers. It was only about an inch and a half long, but I've never liked creepy crawlies since my sleeping bag was filled with daddy long legs for a joke at guide camp in my youth. I chased it across the bed with my book until I stunned it, then scooped it up with a sheet of hotel writing paper and flushed it down the toilet. I put up with bigger spiders at home, but I just couldn't sleep with the thought of a lizard running rampant in the bedroom. Of course my next port of call after Natal is the Amazon, where I suspect I'd see a hell of a lot worse things than midget lizards!

Dunes Adventure: December 24th

I had a great night's sleep, especially considering that I was a little stressed out by the lizard episode. About ten years previously, I'd been on safari in Kenya, and stayed in tree lodges, which were positively crawling with everything imaginable and lots of unimaginable things. My desire to see animals in the wild though was stronger than my fear of creepy crawlies, although in one tree lodge, there were large gaps around the ill-fitting window, and I didn't think I'd be able to sleep with worrying about what was about to attack me. I did of course drift off to sleep, but awoke feeling very stiff as I'd lain in the same position all night. My first thought was "Thank God! I survived!"

The hotel had a small dining room with the décor and ambience of a large farmhouse living kitchen. A delicious spread of cheeses and fruits beckoned me over to the buffet. I ate more than I normally would as I wasn't entirely sure when or what lunch would be, and then I headed to reception for my pick up.

A guy called Washington was ready and waiting. He was huge in both height and girth and must have been somewhere in the region of eighteen stones. His face had the shape and look of a bulldog and was pitted all over with smallpox marks. He was also a little leery and when he spoke it was if he was trying to imagine my naked body at the same time.

"Good morning Suzanna, and what a lovely day we have for a ride in the dunes." His mouth curled ever so slightly at the corners as if he was about to salivate. "May I ask, do you have sun hat and sun block, as it's going to be a really hot day. He emphasised the word "hot" as his eyes looked me up and down.

I could see the jeep through the hotel glass doors and it had a roof, but no sides, so I wasn't going to be too exposed to sun. I walked out and climbed into my seat.

"I always ask my guests," he said, with the smirky smile appearing again "do you want ultimate emotion, lots of emotion or just a little emotion. Thankfully, Junior had explained this to me the previous evening. Otherwise, I may have jumped out of the buggy and given the day a miss. My response to this question would dictate the speed we would drive at and steepness of the sand dunes we would cross.

"I think I should start with just a little emotion, to be on the safe side, and then if it's too tame I could go up a notch." I was hedging my bets because I didn't know what speed he would drive at or what the dunes looked like.

We headed north of Porto Negro where I was staying, towards the city of Natal, using a combination of dirt tracks and road. It was pretty bumpy and I hoped that the dunes would be softer and smoother. We reached a lake where we had to take a ferry across, but this was no usual ferry. Several rafts were waiting by the shore, each one about twice the footprint of the buggy. The ferryman dragged the raft a little onto the sand, and Washington then drove on to it. The ferryman then punted us across the lake.

"It is going to be best to feel the wind in your hair" said Washington as he pulled the roof down. Now I knew why I needed a

90

hat. Although the ferry crossing was included in the tour, I gave the ferryman a small tip.

"It is not long now," drawled Washington, "We'll be at the dunes in about ten minutes."

"Cool!"

"Do you like dancing and going to clubs, because I know some really good ones." Part of me felt that an "invitation" was about to be suggested, so I told him that I hated clubs with a vengeance as they were far too noisy and crowded. This was actually true, and I would go out of my way to avoid them, but I also wanted to make sure he got the message that I wasn't going to be clubbing that evening.

The dunes ride was excellent with the wind indeed gusting through my hair and never being quite sure where Washington was going to turn next. He was driving carefully, and was clearly a skilled navigator of these sandy hillocks. We had a couple of stops for photos, and it was lovely to see the coastline stretching out into the distance, the multi coloured sea, the swaying palm trees and the low rise red roofed buildings of villages up the coast. Not a high rise in sight. However, some of the stops were absolutely geared up for the tourists as there were young beggar children with donkeys posing for photos (for cash) and also options to have a dromedary ride. I declined both saying that I was not a tourist and I didn't like these sorts of things.

Of course I was a tourist, but I liked to think of myself more as an adventurer, and I genuinely didn't, and still don't, like the tacky side of tourism.

We were travelling over the dunes again after a photo stop of an especially picturesque scene, when Washington said to me

"Suzanna, look out to your right and admire the sea." As I did, the buggy lurched over a hill and descended a 1:2 slope very rapidly.

"Oh shit!" I screamed out, as it had come somewhat unexpectedly, and he found it highly amusing as the sea view was obviously the decoy to pull this stunt.

"Was that okay for you Suzanna?"

"Yes, I guess it was, it just came as a bit of a shock."

"I think we can move you up from a little emotion to lots of emotion now" he then pulled away sharply to the left to take in some more dunes. There was nobody in sight at all and the dunes seemed to go on for miles. After the stunt he had pulled, the journey became a lot more exciting and I subconsciously tightened my seat belt

"Are there many accidents in the dunes?" I inquired and he said not.

"I have been driving the dunes for fifteen years and I have never had an accident" he announced proudly, with only a hint of arrogance. It did cross my mind that, if we were to tip over on one of the steep inclines, roll over and I was mangled, whether or not my travel insurance would cover me .

Around mid morning we stopped at a freshwater lagoon. He said that I had forty five minutes there if I wanted to go swimming. I imagined a crystal clear blue lagoon, but it was a bit murky and there are loads of kids splashing about, so I just rested for what turned out to be half an hour with a coke and my book.

Back in the buggy, and more dunes. We stopped at another view point at the top of a dune overlooking another (murky) lagoon, where some zip wires were fixed up and you could go whizzing down into the water. He asked if I wanted to have a go. I declined, not because I was afraid, as I had done zip wiring before and thoroughly enjoyed the exhilaration, but as this one ended in the middle of a murky lagoon, I didn't really want to be wet and smelly for the rest of the day.

We stopped at what effectively was a self-service "dune side" café for lunch. Washington went off to see his mates and left me to eat alone, thankfully. It wasn't that bad for roadside food, but not great either.

After lunch, we headed back to the hotel. On the way back, he told me about other great tours he does and asked if I would like another one tomorrow or Sunday. I asked him for his card and said I'd give him a call if I fancied doing anything. Of course, I had no intention of calling him as his leeriness had surrounded me like a fog throughout the dunes ride. It was only back at the hotel when it crossed my mind of how trusting I was when it comes to these holidays. Alone with a just a guide, I'd been out the previous evening for a meal and a show, and then I'd ridden in a buggy in the middle of the sand dunes without anyone else around, other than a leery buggy driver. Thankfully my belief in human nature being basically decent, had held true. It had been a good fun outing, pretty exciting, and with lovely "paradise" scenery thrown in, so I was glad that I'd taken the trip.

Being hot, sweaty and sandy, I made a beeline for the shower. I was starting to find the heat a little oppressive, yet it was fantastic to just sit on my balcony and take in a little sea breeze. At midday, the temperature had soared to about 45 degrees, but thankfully the humidity was low. So much heat day after day started to make me feel tired and lethargic, however. Gone were the days anyway when I could lie out in the sun at any temperature and not really feel it.

I needed to stretch my legs after being cooped up in the buggy for most of the day, so I trekked up the 45-degree slope from the hotel to the main road and wandered along to the shops to buy some post cards. I had sent some from Iguazu, but as I was now halfway through the holiday I had best send the rest of them to at least give me a chance to return home in advance of the cards.

I had an especially unsatisfactory Christmas Eve dinner. It hadn't occurred to me that I would need to reserve a table, so I just wandered down to the restaurant, which on an evening was effectively tables around the swimming pool. I sat down at one, and was then told by the waiter that not only was it reserved, but that all the tables were reserved. I pointed out that I was staying at the hotel and still needed somewhere to eat.

They found me a little un-set table overlooking the sea so I took that, not that I had any choice. I asked if they had a table lamp as was almost pitch black and I needed to be able to read my book.

"Sorry madam," the waiter said as he sweepingly gestured to the other tables, "they are all used up."

He did however bring me a torch. Although I appreciated this gesture, it was far from ideal, as the beam was quite small so I had to scan each sentence at a time. It was also very windy, which was probably why they hadn't set up any tables in this particular spot. So I was trying to stop the pages from flipping over, whilst holding the torch close enough to the page to illuminate the text, and eat at the same time. I did however work out a way using a tea light holder on the table, to fix the torch so that I could read and finish my meal.

I ordered fish stew, which was effectively bouillabaisse. The menu stated that it was only available for two people so I decided to have it as both my starter and main course. There were quite a few tasty looking options on the menu for "two persons" which was one of the downsides of travelling alone, and a less subtle reminder that you are adventuring solo. It reminded me of a trip to Cyprus some years earlier when I had set out to have a Greek Meze for dinner, lots of little dishes not dissimilar to a having a range of tapas. Restaurant after restaurant would only serve a Meze for two plus people. Some made it clear in their windows, others didn't, and that evening I must have sat down in six restaurants before being told that I couldn't have a Meze. I did eventually find one that would serve me, but the manager clearly wasn't overjoyed at the prospect. Anyway, I really enjoyed this huge Bouillabaisse with the super fresh fish and silky smooth broth.

My table was next to where the sun beds were parked and halfway through the meal, a mother dragged over one of the sun beds right next to my table, so close it was almost touching, and instructed her three year old son Sebastian to lie down on it and go to sleep. (She was speaking in Portuguese, but I followed the conversation.)

"Excuse me," I said, and gestured with my hand to move the sun bed away. She couldn't understand what my problem was, so I gesticulated harder, which very clearly meant "piss off away from my table and let me finish my meal." She moved the sun bed about an inch. Of course the kid didn't settle and was up and down, up and down for the next hour. At the end of their meal, the father and mother each reclined on a sun bed next to the child and then phoned several people to wish them happy Christmas, very loudly. The kid was back around my ankles like a fetid mossie swarm, and the parents could clearly see that he was being a nuisance, yet failed to do anything about it. This wasn't the first time I'd seen evidence of lack of child discipline in Brazil.

Literally, as soon as the meal was over, I retreated to my room. I remembered the lovely Christmas Eve I had spent in Vietnam last year, the tranquillity of the setting and the brightly coloured Chinese lanterns wending their way downstream past the hotel outside a restaurant. The evening I'd just spent was the antithesis of that. I had thought at the time that the Christmas Eve in Vietnam was the best ever, and it remained so.

Although I hadn't had much exercise, the fresh sea air had brought on a veil of lethargy, and I slept like a log.

Christmas Day: December 25th

I awoke and my boobs were killing me, and it didn't take me very long to work out why. Five hours in a buggy going up and down sand dunes, over bumps and rocks would have given someone wearing a sports bra sore breasts, let alone normal attire. I also realised when I looked in a mirror why Washington had been so adamant about me wearing sun block during the buggy ride. My face was redder than a beetroot and glowing like a throbbing plum.

It looked like it was going to be a cloudy day as I stepped onto the balcony but it was still pretty humid too. I took my coffee out and the phone rang. In moving inside with the coffee in my hand, I managed to leave a trail of spilt coffee across the tiled floor - damn. It was George calling to wish me happy Christmas. We only chatted for a couple of moments, but it was good to hear a friendly voice.

I went down to breakfast and saw the father from the sun bed incident last night with whom was presumably his older son, a thirteen or fourteen years old boy, grossly overweight and carrying a mean scowl around his face. He moved around the tables with a swagger, eyeing all the food as if it was prey. He piled his plate to overflowing and even when he was walking back to his table, he was looking over his shoulder scanning the rest of the buffet, already deciding what he'd have for subsequent courses. I couldn't ever imagine this kid smiling and he had the look of a bully about him. Yep, if you spoil your kids and don't discipline them then this is potentially how they turn out. I suspected that little Sebastian from last night would pretty much go the same way.

So, what was I to do with myself on Christmas day in Natal? Had the sun been out I'd have sunbathed for a while on the balcony even though the searing heat definitely made me feel sluggish. I needed to leave the room to allow housekeeping in, so I wandered up to the shops to see if anything was open. I was half hoping the souvenir market would be open, and it was, so I spent an hour or so wandering around the stalls, admiring the local crafts (and cringing at others). It wasn't busy, so I stopped and chatted to some of the stallholders, to some in English, some in Portunol English, and others with sign language. They were all friendly and welcoming, and not one of them tried any hard sell on me. The only thing I was actually looking for was a napkin holder. The hotel had them on the tables. Very simple wooden blocks with a fish shaped wooden weight that pressed down on paper napkins to stop them from blowing away. I quite fancied getting a couple of those for my infrequent barbecues back home and I was in luck. I also bought a wind charm for my garden, made from slivers of polished stone, and then I saw a stone ornament of a Brazilian chap playing the accordion. It was a stunning and well carved piece, but weighed a ton and I worried about both my suitcase allowance and the ability to get it home without it breaking, so I ignored it and wandered round the rest of the stalls. Somehow, I gravitated back to the stone ornament and I bought it. Instantly I started making excuses in my head to placate myself, yet it wasn't expensive, only thirty five Reals which was about £9. The shopkeeper wrapped it up very carefully for me.

Whilst heading back to the entrance, on impulse I bought another napkin holder for Joe as it was the sort of thing he'd like. Then at the entrance, where there was a jewellery stall, I bought myself two necklaces for a total of £7, which was really quite ridiculous as I hardly ever wear jewellery.

I headed back to the hotel pretty pleased with my purchases, and conned myself that they were Christmas presents for me. I had only got one present before I left home and that was another Laaf from Joe. I had opened it before I came away. Laaf's are ceramic figures of hobbit like creatures, about eighteen inches high, in different poses. I loved them. The detail is extremely intricate, down to darn marks in their socks. They are the sort of figures you could imagine coming alive when everyone is asleep, fooling around and then going back to their poses as the household awakens. I think they appeal to the "cute" side of me.

Back at the ranch I logged on to see if there were any Christmas greetings from anyone. There was an e-mail from Tony, who apologised for not writing sooner but had been very much wrapped up with the new love in his life, which was great news.

I also had an email from Stephen, which started "Hi Prosperously Unemployed Kid". This made me laugh. He said that he was not in the least bit Christmassy, but unbeknown to him, by this amusing start to the email, he had sent some Christmas cheer to Brazil.

At lunchtime, I didn't feel hungry so decided to have a couple of beers on the balcony and do some topless sunbathing, even though the sun wasn't out. It occasionally appeared from behind the clouds, so I reckoned that with the sea breeze it would be quite pleasant to sit out. I was still reading Money by Martin Amis. Initially I had found it almost as depressing as "London Fields" that I had read before the holiday. The language was bad and there was a lot about pornography and perversion, and I was about to give up on it, but decided to persevere. I then become hooked and indeed hardly put it down until it was finished. Despite the raunchy parts, it also had lashings of dry humour and I decided not to leave this book in the hotel room, but to take it home to read again at some point in the future.

At about teatime, I staggered in from the balcony. The sun may not have been out much, but I'd certainly caught it.

I dined on shrimp soup and then fettuccine, but as the soup was so filling I ate less than a third of the pasta.

Before retiring for the night, I logged on and ordered a get well card from Moonpig for Stephen who was about to have a hand operation. I found the appropriate section and I wanted to find a humorous one. The selection wasn't that great but I came across one that was a little bit smutty, but very amusing, so I selected that, personalised it, added a message, his address and then hit send. He should get it Saturday and, hopefully, it would bring a small smile to his face as the anaesthetic was wearing off

I wasn't at all comfortable with these laid-back-do-nothing-today holidays. I became too restless and would have much preferred to be out exploring, so I had an early night and was asleep by 22:00.

Rest and Relaxation: December 26th

Having gone to bed early, I was up around 06:00, so I had my coffee on the balcony and carried on reading "Money."

I planned to have a late breakfast, no lunch and an early dinner as my pick up the next day was at 04:00.

I ventured a little further than usual on my walk out and found a stall selling packets of Brazilian coffee and bought a suitable number of packets for the folks back home. Unfortunately the coffee bean bags were large and heavy whereas the ground beans were much smaller and lighter. Although Junior had told me that Brazilians don't know how to make coffee they just grow the beans, my friends were going to have the cafeteria version, and in any case, it's the thought that counts! It suddenly struck me that I didn't need to take any sweets or goodies back for the office staff as I wouldn't be seeing them again, so to celebrate I bought another necklace. I couldn't understand what this sudden fascination with buying necklaces was, I'm hardly a "jewellery" person, and I put it down to restlessness as I was ready to move on to my next adventure.

I picked up my emails and one was from Joe, who was now back home after a couple of days at his girlfriends', so I gave him a call to wish him happy Christmas. He said that he fought against Christmas as best he could, having kippers for breakfast and soup for lunch, absolutely determined not to succumb, and had even volunteered to do lots of little DIY jobs for Penny to avoid ending up on the sofa watching the reiterative perfunctory Christmas movies.

101

"I'm knackered after a couple of days of DIY, but it was worth it to avoid the silly season."

"So what are you planning to do now that you are back home?" I ventured.

"As little as possible for as long as possible." He wasn't joking.

"I just don't understand how you can do so little on a day-to-day basis. I've just had two days of rest and have been tearing my hair out."

"I'd hardly call a dune buggy ride having a day of rest!" He laughed.

"It was just half a day, and I'm more that ready for the next part of my journey."

"I've lost track of your itinerary, where is next?"

"The Amazon. Tomorrow I go to the Amazon!"

"Well good luck, and watch out for the piranhas," he quipped.

"Will do. Take care, and an early 'happy New Year' to you. I won't be able to make contact in the Amazon, so I'll see you at the other side."

"Bah humbug," he laughed as he put the phone down.

I spent the remainder of the afternoon on the balcony and finished reading Money and then got the next book out. I dozed off for a couple of hours between books. I really didn't like this chilling out and was just itching for the next day.

I returned to the seafood restaurant along the promenade for dinner to have another of their excellent seafood pizzas. It was only about 17:00, but I wanted to have an early dinner and furthermore I didn't want to have to walk back along the promenade too long after dark.

As I walked along the promenade I saw an extraordinary number of petting couples. I wondered how long it had been since I was kissed, and whether I would remember how to do it should the opportunity avail itself in the future.

The pizza, as expected, was excellent and I was glad I'd returned to this restaurant. I sat looking out to sea as the new moon rose on the horizon, large, orange and low. I wished I'd taken my camera with me as the phenomenon was stunning. I stared at it for several minutes and actually watched it rising into the sky. It was especially beautiful with the moonlight glistening on the rippling water.

The walk back along the promenade wasn't at all scary and there were still plenty of people around so I didn't feel too unsafe. I passed one young couple sitting on the seawall, enveloped in each other and he was gently brushing her hair from her face. It brought tears to my eyes when I realised that this was what I missed most of all being single and that was just being touched. There were times when I could murder for a hug, for example the night Misty died.

By the time I reached the hotel the moon was looking more or less normal, so no point rushing for my camera. I settled my hotel bill and packed for the next part of the journey, the next day would be a very early start, even by my standards.

From Beach to Jungle: December 27th

As suspected I didn't get much sleep and was wide awake at 00:00, 01:00 and 02:00. I was worried about missing the alarm call, plus I was excited to be back on the adventure. I decided that I may as well get up and ready, as I clearly wasn't going to get any quality sleep, so I did, which was just as well, as the early morning call I'd booked for 03:15 never came.

My boobs were sore again that morning, not because of the buggy riding, I had been topless sunbathing on my balcony when I had dozed off for a couple of hours the previous afternoon and I think my nipples got sunburnt.

A female tour guide picked me up from the hotel and the flight to Brasilia was fine. The flight wasn't busy and I managed to find three empty seats together and was able to get about an hour and a half kip.

At Brasilia airport I checked my watch, 09:30. My flight to Manaus wasn't until 10:40, so I reckoned that I had time to nip out of the terminal, have a ciggie, change some money and buy an extra insect spray in case I ran out in the Amazon. I couldn't find anywhere to change money which wasn't really surprising as I was in their domestic terminal, so I wandered back in slowly towards the gate. I was looking for my flight on the board, when I noticed that the board said that the actual time was 10:45. I checked my watch and it only read 09:45, then I thought SHIT! There must have been a one hour time difference and because all the announcements on the plane were in Portuguese I missed it. I ran to the gate with super human timing expecting to see my plane taxiing down the runway, but the gate was still open, and indeed they were waiting for one more plane to land which held people who were transferring to Manaus. Gosh, that was damned lucky. I'd always wondered how people who had checked their luggage in managed to fail to turn up at the plane for departure. Then of course there follows the inevitable delay whilst their luggage has to be unloaded. I was determined to have more sympathy for them in the future, as a simple hour's change in the clock and a minimal or zero understanding of the local language could cause it.

The flight to Manaus was uncomfortable. There wasn't much leg room, and I swear if the person in front of me had put their chair back any further they'd have been resting their head in my lap.

The guide was waiting for me, and I was whisked off to the resort. The first part of the journey was by mini bus to a small port, then we had to take a little boat down the river for twenty minutes, and I mean a little boat.

Initially the surroundings didn't look like jungle to me, and I was a little disappointed as I recalled all the childhood picture books about the Amazon, which had no doubt fired up my desire to visit the area, but once we got away from the airport, roads and Manaus, it became jungle, and I couldn't stop grinning.

The boat took us down river and there was a floating houseboat with one elderly gentleman who acted as a "sentry" to the resort. He waved when he saw us approaching and as we passed he picked up a piece of rope that he pulled up across the river to say "no access". The boat stopped at a floating platform and as we climbed out I was told, by sign language, to leave my luggage as it would be brought up later.

I walked along the floating platform which bobbed gently and rhythmically in the lagoon, and then there was a steep incline up the sandbank to the Amazon Eco Resort.

I was given a most welcome, welcome drink and then the keys to my hut. It was number 15C and towards the back of the resort, with quite a walk through the jungle along a narrow, gravely prepared path. Iguanas were padding across the walkway, there were ants the size of large spiders and about a million different noises of insects and creatures caterwauling around me.

I walked very slowly, partly to take in the surroundings and partly because I didn't want to walk too fast and bump into, or step onto, "something".

I reached my wooden hut and it was somewhat primordial. The first thing I noticed was the corrugated metal roof, and the ill-fitting windows. Inside there was no telephone line, which didn't surprise me, so as expected I'd just have to be out of touch with the world for a few days. There was no television either so I felt a shiver of excitement that I was out in the jungle, not knowing what was going on in the world nor being able to contact anyone. Yeah, this was a great adventure, much better than chilling out in Natal. I had enjoyed Natal, it was just that I wasn't cut out for more than half a day of relaxation. When I was checking in I had heard an American saying that he needed to make a call to America and where would he find the nearest phone. The response was "Manaus" as they only used mobile phones at the resort, and these were only available for guest use in a genuine emergency.

Before exploring further I needed to do a full check of the room. You may think that this was an easy task, as the room was only about twelve feet square and the bathroom was simple with a loo, wash basin and shower, all encased in cracked and broken tiles, but this was a lizard and creepy crawly check, as I didn't want any nasty surprises in the night, which meant that I would examine every nook and cranny with the dedication of a forensic scientist. The room checked out and seemed to be lizard and large insect free, but there was a gap under the entrance door which could worryingly let in all kinds of unwelcome creatures. I stuffed one of the towels into the gap just to be sure. There was absolutely no point unpacking anything because although it was slightly cooler than Natal, around 28 degrees, it was immensely humid, so the more I left out, the more it would get damp. The final thing before leaving the room was to plug in my electric mosquito repellent and I slid a new tablet onto the heated element. That would at least keep the room mozzie free.

It was only about 13:45 and the tour guide had told me to meet at 15:30 for the first boat trip, so I had some lunch. This was served in the main room, which was a large wooden circular structure with no sides and a palm leaf roof. Everything was included at the Eco Resort, except drink, so I helped myself to the buffet, which was mainly fish and salad. Throughout lunch I could hear an older American guy yak yakking at a thousand decibels to a young English couple about all the places they must get to see in the world, yak yak yak. His wife, who has been silent up to this point - possibly because she couldn't get a word in edgeways, wandered over to a waiter and asked for a cup of coffee granules only. She didn't want a made up coffee, just the granules. The poor waiter didn't understand what she wanted, and she was obviously one of those people who believed that if you raised your voice and shouted out the request, in what was a foreign language to the recipient, they would suddenly become bilingual and understand. After I'd heard this request half dozen times, I walked over and asked if I could help (anything to shut her up) and she explained that she wanted some coffee granules because there was a smell in their room and a bowl of coffee granules (apparently) absorbs smells. I turned to the waiter and said in Portunol, "she would like a cup with coffee but no water please." He understood, and went off and brought her what she wanted. Astonishing. I didn't really speak the language, yet I had become a translator. It dawned on me that if you had to live in a foreign land by necessity sake, and had only a very basic grasp of the language, you could actually pick it up, or at least make yourself understood, pretty quickly.

After lunch I sat in the "lobby", which was another open to the elements construction near the dining area with a palm leaf roof, and waited for the afternoon tour.

The tours were very well organised. Most people did the same four day tour as I did, and you were put with a guide and a group speaking the same language. The groups were purposely kept small and mine was comprised of a couple of Americans, a couple of Dutch people, a chap from I didn't know where and an elderly Swiss lady, but the tour was to be in English. The trips were just repeated, so you joined wherever in the programme, and some of the people I was with had already done two or three days.

We were introduced to Antonio who was to be our guide. He was around forty years old, a native Amazonian and spoke excellent English. He led us down to the little harbour and we clambered into one of the small boats, which in fact was the same one that had brought me from Manaus. This trip was to visit a local village and on the way back to hopefully spot some crocodiles.

"We welcome Suzanne who has joined our little family," said Antonio, and we all introduced ourselves. This was the last day for most of them, although only the second day for the Swiss lady, Camille. "This afternoon," he continued, "we are going to visit a typical Amazonian village, where I will explain many things to you about the way we live, and if we are lucky, we may see some crocodiles also."

The boat took us up through one of the tributaries, and I just gazed at the surroundings, taking it all in. Ultra lush greenery, birds chattering away in the trees, swampy mangrove sides to some of the banks and the slightly murky brown water of the river. The mangrove bushes were amazing with their multitude of tendril like roots anchoring to the river floor.

"We are at the beginning of the winter season," Antonio explained, "and the river is relatively low, but even so, you can see several trees and bushes growing out of the water. The vegetation in this area quite varied, from tall palm trees and dense jungle foliage to shorter, mangrove swamp type bushes." As we passed each minor tributary my eyes searched hopefully for the sight of a crocodile, but to no avail.

After about half an hour we pulled into the side, and alighted for a jungle walk to a village. It was quite hot and sticky and some of the route a little precarious with the path being muddy and having a plank across it, or a sudden large dip in the ground that you had to stride over, but suddenly we emerged in a semi clearing which revealed the village.

"The way it works out here," Antonio said, "is that that six or seven families will set up home together in one area. This particular village had a school built two years ago. The families have between six and thirteen children."

"Thirteen?" I gasped.

"Yes, it is not unknown. I myself come from a family of fifteen." He smiled and then continued "I guess that before television arrived, the only thing they had to do in the evenings was make babies."

We stopped in the centre of the clearing where buildings on stilts were perched around the edges. Some, like the church, were painted white and blue, others were just natural wood.

"The children go to the school from three to sixteen. The parents could send them to a "proper" school in Manaus, and there is a boat that could take them in once a week, however, they fear their children mixing with "town kids" and getting into drugs and the like, so they prefer to educate them in the village. The elders will select half a dozen bright kids and send them on a teacher training course in Manaus, then those who pass, and want to return to the village, become the teachers. They teach pretty much the full age span, sometimes all in the same classroom."

Some little boys were playing with the jungle equivalent of a "remote controlled toy car". They were plastic cars about a foot long, with a piece of string attached to the front and this in turn was attached to a stick, which the boys used to manoeuvre the toys.

We were shown some handicrafts that villagers had made for passing tourists to raise a little extra cash. There was not much on display, a couple of beaded necklaces and some darts for poison arrows, without the poison. I bought one of these, more as a token to the village and as a thank you for letting us see it, than as a desired souvenir.

The standard of living here was clearly quite basic, yet they all looked happy. Antonio explained that he was raised in such an environment, a native Indian two hundred miles from Manaus.

"Although it may look a little idyllic, you know, living off the land and being free to do what you want, it's a very tough existence. In this village, last year a mother died leaving children, including a little girl of one year old, because the woman had diabetes, and they just didn't know how to treat it. Then there are other dangers such as snakebites. They are too far from Manaus to be able to get help in time." I was impressed with the quality of his English, and almost as if he had read my mind he continued.

"I learned English at school, because I thought this would be a way to improve myself. After school I took a job shovelling cement to fund myself through college and then became a teacher, but I didn't like it, so I took a job as a receptionist in a hotel. Whilst I was there an elderly English gentleman befriended me, and encouraged me in my learning English. This guy became like a second father to me and I was invited to go and stay at the gentleman's house up the river. Whilst I was there the gentleman asked me to guide a group of a dozen tourists. I freaked at this, because I was quite shy. I was used to speaking with tourists on a one-to-one basis over the counter of the hotel, but to be suddenly asked to guide a group of twelve. I thought it would be a nightmare. However, that was the start of my life as a tour guide, and I ran some more tours for my second dad. Sadly the guy returned to England and died in tragic circumstances. I then applied for a job at the Amazon Eco resort. I have now been here for nineteen years. I love the work, but my dream is to run my own tour group company." We never found out what the tragic circumstances were, but there were indications in subsequent conversations that it may have been a car accident.

We discovered throughout the trip that because he was brought up in the jungle he was incredibly knowledgeable about all the plants, animals and ways of living. This along with his almost perfect English made him one of the best guides I had ever had, and indeed that still rings true today as none have come anywhere near his high standard since.

On the way back to the boat, a teenage girl ran up to us and put red paint on our cheeks like war paint. Then two little native girls came up to me, each taking one of my hands. I looked back at the others in the tour group and said "but I'm allergic!" Of course these two little girls were absolute cuties and as they were about to leave me, they asked if I have any "bonbons". I didn't, the only thing I had with me was a packet of Airways chewing gum, but I took out the packet, split it in half and give each girl half a packet. I demonstrated that it was chewing gum so that they didn't swallow it or choke on it and Antonio explained to them in Tupi, their local language, so that there was no chance of them thinking it was an ordinary sweet. One of the girls started flapping at her mouth. They had obviously never tried anything as strong as Airways, which is so called because it clears out the nasal passages.

"I'm sorry girls, but it's the only sweets I have with me." I did however have some biros with me, as I always carried them while on holiday should I need to give little gifts. They are lightweight, inexpensive, easy to take a large bundle and always of use to the recipient. I delved into my rucksack and produced a couple of pens. The girls spat out the chewing gum, grabbed the pens and danced up and down smiling.

It was starting to get dark, so Antonio said that we would head back to the Eco resort, but would look for crocodiles on the way, but we were more likely to see caiman, the little crocodile.

"The way to spot them," explained Antonio, "is to shine a light around, and their eyes show as yellowish red lights. You then head out towards them, and catch them. Easy, see."

We'd been looking for crocs for about half an hour, when Antonio said something to the young lad steering the boat, and he killed the engine. We floated in the shallow swamps, all of us holding our breath in case we made a sound. By this time it was absolutely pitch black, but Antonio could spot a croc anywhere. We drifted towards the bank, and were somewhat disconcerted when Antonio suddenly stepped out of the boat into the water, not something I'd do in a croc-infested piranha rich river. He moved slowly and there was total silence. He bent down carefully, put his hands in the water and hey presto, came up suddenly with a baby croc about two feet long. He moved alongside the boat to show it to everyone, grinning as if to say "told you it was easy!"

"I fink that you are vewy brave," said Camille.

"Not at all," Antonio said as he shook his head. "This is just a baby. They become dangerous once they are over a metre long. It's their tails that do the damage, whipping the prey towards their mouths. Crocs work on the basis of grabbing hold and pulling flesh off one piece at a time." We shivered as Antonia raised his trouser leg a few inches showing us the scar where he'd been bitten by a croc about two metres long.

"I was out with a group of German tourists, and I stepped into the water. I had seen the large crocodile and I straddled it with my legs as I was planning to grip it round its neck to raise it up from the water to show the tourists. However, the riverbed was silty and my feet sank with one leg either side of the croc. I tried to gently manoeuvre away from it, but it swung its head and bit me on the leg. I was very lucky that I was between the head and the tail so it

115

couldn't sweep me totally round to his mouth, otherwise I'd have lost my leg. I then grasped the croc with my arms around his neck and pulled it out of the water for the tourists to see. It was a dark night and very black, and the only thing the tourists saw was me with the croc and they cheered and started taking photographs. It was not until we got back to the Eco resort and we were in the light that they saw my injury. They hadn't realised I'd been bitten." That really was dedication to his work, as he had about a six inches deep scar on his inside thigh, so how he had managed to get back to the resort without anyone knowing was simply astonishing. A real life Crocodile Dundee.

As we returned to the resort, we all became experts at spotting crocs, because when the beam of light was shone around the banks, you could see their eyes. When we were almost back, we saw a croc coming towards us. Antonio waved for the boat boy to stop as we glided towards the croc. He studied it carefully as we approached, put his hand in the water and then with a swoop, caught the croc. It was about six inches longer than the baby one we'd seen earlier, but he was so chuffed to have caught two during the trip. Another tour boat out croc-spotting was now also returning to the resort but hadn't seen any close up, and their guide certainly hadn't caught any. Antonio whistled them over and handed his second croc over to them to look at.

After the croc hunting we returned to base for dinner. By this time, I was so sweaty I thought my clothes would walk off me, but I went straight into dinner as the welcoming smell of the food was more tempting than going back to my shack for a shower. It was a buffet affair again, and very similar to lunch. There was an amazing atmosphere at this place. It was like a giant camp, very relaxed and informal, with the guides mingling with the tourists. There were set meal times and the trips were organised around those. It was a jungle canteen.

Not wanting to see, or caring, if there were lizards in my hut when I returned, I consumed four beers. With the early start and time changes, it was effectively as if I'd been up since 01:00 local time so I was pretty tired and retired to my hut shortly after finishing the meal. The huts were placed about one hundred yards apart, set back from the main track, so I had to walk quite some distance to reach mine. The Eco Park had been exceptionally well designed so each hut was away from the others, giving the feel of being alone in the jungle.

Once inside I did a lizard check. Nothing, but I pushed a towel against the crack at the bottom of the door again, just to be certain. I really wanted to crawl under the shower, but I was so tired, and didn't care that I was covered in sticky mosquito repellent and dust, so I just stripped off and got into bed dirty.

I always liked a bit of light when staying in a strange new place, so I lit a candle and drifted off to sleep. The bed had a duvet cover and then a sheet. Having been so hot this holiday I just used the sheet. However, the old rattling air conditioning unit was surprisingly very effective, and the temperature was dropping quite sharply at night. I was awake a couple of hours later absolutely freezing. I tried to snuggle down under the sheet, but it was no use, so I gave in and retrieved the duvet. I quickly fell asleep again and survived the first night, totally oblivious to any creepy crawlies that may have managed to get past Fort Knox and into my room.

The Meeting of the Rivers: December 28th

Having survived my first day and night in the jungle, I had a lot more confidence as I strolled along to the restaurant for breakfast. I had a sore bum from sitting for about five hours on a basic wooden plank in a boat, and made a mental note to take a towel to sit on for any other boat trips.

Breakfast was quite basic, and I had an omelette and bread, before we gathered at 08:30 for our full day trip down the river.

It was a two-deck boat, mainly covered, but I got myself a good position on the upper deck in full sunshine. It was a beautiful day with pretty much clear blue skies. A woman who had been on this particular trip a couple of days before, had told me over breakfast that it had rained all day for her and that the rain was freezing, so nobody had enjoyed the trip very much. There wasn't a cloud in sight so I doubted that I'd get a drop of rain, and I didn't. Guess it's luck of the draw when you take a trip, and if you are on a schedule, you can't really wait around for a fine day to come along.

The journey down river took about three hours to get to where the river Negro meets the river Solimoes and becomes the river Amazon.

The trip took us past Manaus where there was a tremendous amount of shipbuilding all along the banks. There were also some favelas, the poor quarters, where the houses looked as if they have been built on top of each other. It was lovely just watching the world go by, taking in the local scenery. I was quite amused to see a

119

floating petrol station, still, I guess the boats had to fuel up somewhere, although I expected a refuelling boat-type tanker, not what looked like a floating ESSO station.

The meeting of the rivers was incredible. One of those sights you have to personally witness to realise that it's true and not an illusion. The River Negro is black and has an acidic PH and a warm temperature. The Solimoes, on the other hand, is brown, cooler and more alkaline in nature. As a result, the two rivers don't mix and you can see an almost straight line where the two rivers join to create the Amazon. It was without doubt one of the most stunning natural phenomena I had ever seen.

The boat hovered around the line for ten minutes so that we could all take photographs and then we continued down the Amazon and towards a small village for lunch.

The village houses, like the village I had seen the day previously, were on stilts, because the Amazon can rise about another four feet from where it was currently.

Antonio asked us whether we wanted to do an optional trip after lunch and go piranha fishing. I said that I'd go along for the trip to watch, but didn't especially want to fish.

The lunch was in a mud hut affair with open sides. A smaller version of the one back at the resort, and there was a sumptuous buffet laid out for us. I started with piranha soup which was excellent. There were about six or seven different fish on the cold

120

buffet table and a couple more on the warm buffet table, and I sampled them all, and they were excellent also.

The gardens around the restaurant boasted banana trees, vibrant red Heliconia and Cocoa trees. Antonio picked one of the pods and split it open for us to see the white fleshy insides.

After lunch we went piranha fishing on a lake nearby. two people did indeed catch piranhas, and several of the others catfish, but I could never take up angling as to me it was worse than sitting and watching paint dry. Still at least I got to see a live piranha, and, even more impressive than catching a crocodile, Antonio took the piranha off the lines, gripped their mouths to show us the razor sharp teeth, and then returned them to the water.

It was then back to the main boat for the three hour journey back to the hotel. As it was still pretty hot, I sat up on the top deck and watched the world go by.

I changed into light trousers and top for the evening, partly because of the temperature drop, but also because my shorts were desperate for a laundry visit after two days in the Amazon, but there were no laundry facilities other than the river, and that, on balance, looked muddier than my shorts. I was going to have to wait now until I got to my next destination.

It was another pleasant dinner, although identical to the lunch and dinner the previous day. Even though I had worn long trousers, and put mozzie repellent around my ankles, something managed to get up my right trouser leg, so when I got back to the room it looked like my legs had measles. The new insect repellent I'd bought at the airport was great, like liquid citronella, so perhaps the mozzie was in my trousers before I put them on.

Jungle Walk: December 29th

Yeah! A second night survived in the jungle! During the night there had been tremendous thunderstorms and everything was wet but fresh and the glossy evergreens were shimmering like cascading emeralds. At least the rain came during the night as this morning's excursion was a jungle walk.

After breakfast, with strong shoes and full length trousers, we headed into the jungle. Antonio never ceased to amaze me and he was an amaranthine mine of information. He knew all the plants, all the trees, which ones were medicinal, which ones are poisonous. There seemed to be no end to his depth of knowledge. Sometimes you can get a guide who knows his subject inside out, but has either not enough English to do it justice or lacks the charismatic personality to bring it alive. Sometimes you can get an excellent English speaking guide, but their depth of knowledge and ability to answer any questions thrown at them is negligible. If you are really lucky you may find a guide who has good English and a reasonable depth of knowledge, but fails to inspire as they sound like they are regurgitating a text book. With Antonio we had everything.

We passed a trail of black ants, and Antonio stopped to look at them.

"We use these for men who are unfaithful to their wives," he revealed. "The black ants are put in two bags, and then the man has his hands plunged into the bags which are then tied around his wrists and left there for many minutes. Their bite doesn't kill, but it's very painful and makes you ill." We looked to see if he was smiling

123

or pulling our legs, but this was a serious piece of information he was imparting.

"I was once bitten by just four of these ants and was sick for a fortnight, so an errant husband has a lot to fear. I have always been, and will remain faithful to my wife." We laughed, but Antonio continued solemnly, "but that is because I love her, not because I am afraid of ants." We followed Antonio deeper into the jungle and he stopped by a palm tree, where many fronds were freshly strewn around following the storms during the night.

"These are very useful trees for us," he said as he cut a couple fresh branches from the tree. "But we have to be careful how many trees we use, because worldwide demand for palm oil continues to increase and if we are not careful, we will have no trees left. Because palm oil has a high melting point, this makes it smooth and easy to spread, and you find it in lots of products; food, cosmetics, detergents and candles, to name just a few examples. We use the leaves to thatch our roofs, and we also make baskets by weaving them. They have a fun element too, and we make ornaments for our houses and toys for the children." At this point he drew out a sharp knife from his belt and started cutting and scraping at one of the leaves, then replaced the knife and started twisting the fronds. Within two minutes he had made a superb locust which he proudly presented to Camille who held it up so that we could photograph it. Exquisite jungle origami.

"Come everyone, let's walk further, but keep a good look out for snakes, as we may see some today, especially after the rain last night." We heard a rustle behind us and we jumped, but it was a colleague of Antonio. Antonio spoke to him briefly then turned to us.

"Fabio is going to show you how we collect palm oil in the jungle. This is the traditional way, although obviously big plantations have more modern mechanical means." Fabio was already halfway up the tree, shimmying up using a leather belt around the trunk that he held at each end. He would get a grip with his knees and feet, move the belt up a little, then move his legs a few inches higher. He did this very quickly so that he was thirty feet up in a matter of seconds. He drew a small pouch and a knife from his pocket and sliced into the bark, catching the palm sap in the pouch. When he returned to the ground he flung his small backpack over his shoulder and I could see a spear and blow pipe strapped to the side. He joined us for the remainder of the walk.

The further we walked, the more dense the jungle became and the taller the trees.

"The soil next to the river, by the Eco park, is very poor quality, and not rich with nutrients, so very little grows tall. That is why when people first arrive, they are a little disappointed that it doesn't look like the jungle they expected from the television. But once you get even half a mile from the river, the land is much more fertile and that's where you can see the tall jungle trees. You wouldn't have to walk more than a mile before the path becomes too difficult to navigate, and if you don't know where you are going, you would easily get lost."

We came to a small clearing with a little pond, around which were half a dozen giant turtle. As if reading our minds, Fabio approached one of them and gently placed his foot on the shell so that we could take a photography that reflected the true size of these stunning creatures. A picture of a turtle without perspective could have been three inches or three feet in length. These were close to three feet.

Back to the Eco Park, I had time for a quick shower before lunch. As I passed one of the other huts, I heard the cleaning lady squeal followed by a lot of broom battering. I dread to think what she found in that room, especially considering that living here she must have encountered most creatures at one time or another.

I was about to sit down at a table when I noticed an unwanted guest. A snake had just slithered up the leg of the table and was making its way across the surface.

"Hey everyone!" I shouted, "come and have a look at this." Others left their lunches to come and see. Antonio pushed forward and said,

"There is no need to worry, this is just a baby."

"Just a baby?" I exclaimed, "but it is about three feet long."

"It is still only a baby. It is a boa constrictor. Let it continue on its journey." I photographed it and then sat at a different table.

After lunch I had the massage that I booked the previous evening. Full body for an hour. It was extremely relaxing to the point

126

that I hardly wanted to go out in the afternoon as I could have quite easily fallen asleep for the rest of the day.

I still had a couple of hours before the next excursion, so I strolled around the resort, where I saw several parrots. There were two beautiful green ones, eying each other lovingly and in one area there were two large brightly coloured birds, one blazing red and the other kingfisher blue. There was a hand written sign near them saying "nesting parrots, please do not go too near". I followed the request.

I bought some tropical fruit juice and sat in one of the rattan arm chairs around the edge of the dining area, and pondered for a while. I really, really loved the Amazon, which surprised me considering my nervousness about the creepy crawlies and other potential large nasties. When I had visited Kenya, and especially the tree house hotels open to the elements, I was frankly scared shitless, I'd told myself that my desire to see animals in the wild was stronger than my fear of the insects, snakes and other creatures I could encounter. There had been moths with each wing the size of a man's hand, hanging from the ceiling of the washrooms, and to me it was a terrifying gauntlet just to get to the loo. In the evening there were rhinoceros beetles the size of a fist scurrying around the floor, yet throughout, my desire to wait in the semi -darkness to watch leopards drinking from the pond was worth it. For some reason, I had expected the Amazon to be ten times worse, yet it wasn't, and everything I had seen so far moved slowly enough for me to keep out of its way.

The trips so far had been absolutely phantasmagorical. Even the fact that I was staying in very basic accommodation made it more exciting and authentic. I knew that I was getting "strength" from the Amazon, and I thought about the old tribes of large, strong women who were leaders of their clans and whom I'd read about as a child. I knew that there was some debate about whether these women were myths, legends or had indeed had existed at all, but I wanted to believe it. According to Antonio there were none of these tribes left now and indeed had been extinct for some four hundred years. However, he said, there are still tribes in the heart of the jungle that know nothing about modern life, and effectively had yet to be "discovered".

"It is possible to take a trip up river and visit some remote tribes," he had said, "however it is very, very expensive, it takes about two weeks, and you are not allowed to take a camera with you. For this reason there are not many tourists who do such trips. It is left to the explorers and anthropologists."

This feeling of emotional strength gained in the Amazon, has stayed with me, and I was able to harness its power twelve months later when attending an NLP training course. One of the exercises was to create your personal "power mat". These were subconscious mats that we could hypothetically throw on the floor, step on and take from them whatever power we had created with them. The way they were created was as follows. First of all, you had to think of a power that you wanted to harness. As I had embarked on my own consultancy I wanted the power of confidence and the strength of character when facing potential new business clients. You then stood with your eyes closed and imagined throwing a rug onto the floor. It could be any shape or colour you wanted. Mine was a green oval one, the same green as the lush vegetation of the Amazon after a storm. With your eyes still closed, you physically stepped forward on to your mat with your arms hanging loose at your sides. You then had to imagine where you were, a place that evoked the powers you wanted to harness. I was back in the Amazon. You then had to repeat in your head, a phrase that summarised the power you were calling upon. Mine was "I am tall, strong and powerful". You silently repeated this phrase whilst standing on the invisible mat and feeling with every sense that you were in the place that had made you feel this way. After a while, I could physically feel strength creeping up my legs and into my body. I felt physically taller, but most importantly, I felt that I could tackle anything. This exercise was repeated several times so that the power you were seeking became hardwired into your psyche. Once there, all you had to do, at any time you needed it, was to mentally throw your mat on the floor, step onto it and say to yourself "I am tall, strong and powerful" and the feeling of power was there in an instant. I have lost count of how many times I have used my power mat. Before important pitches, before making a major business presentation and before making life changing decisions. Sometimes when I was heading to London for a significant business meeting, I would stand on Wendover station platform and take sixty seconds out to access my power mat and prepare myself psychologically for the meeting ahead. So if you were a Wendover commuter and thought you saw a strange woman who momentarily took a step forward and went into a brief trance, then that was me.

129

The afternoon trip was another boat excursion, but this time a little further down the tributary to see the monkeys. I was surprised that they were so relatively close to the hotel yet kept their distance, as monkeys usually congregate around tourists because they know they are a source of food.

Antonio had brought a camera with him.

"I don't have a camera myself, because I have never had need. I see crocodiles every day and I am very familiar with the jungle and rivers in this area. My pictures are in my head. However, I want to develop a web site to promote my own tours, so today I have borrowed a camera from a friend to hopefully get some action shots. Will you take some photos for me?"

"Yes, certainly." I agreed. To start off with, he passed me the camera at appropriate moments and asked me to take a photo, where he would stand tall in front of a luscious plant, or crouch next to an iguana, but after a while we were on the same wave length and he either just passed it to me or I held my hand out for it when I saw a "photo opportunity" coming on. He reciprocated by taking pictures of me with my camera.

As soon as we landed on the monkey beach, one friendly monkey came running over and started jumping up at people. He was really cute and totally harmless, so when he jumped up at me, I picked him up. I then had him crawling over my head, down my back, round my side and down my leg. As we left the beach area, there were two other types of monkey, the red faced and the black monkey who remained in the tree branches watching us carefully.

Most of the monkeys were friendly, presumably because they were used to seeing visitors in this part of the jungle, although the red monkey took some coaxing down from a tree by Antonio with a brazil nut. I went over to a black monkey sitting at the base of a palm tree and stroked him, which he allowed, and didn't jump up at me. I then remembered that I had half a bag of cashew nuts in my backpack, in case I got the munchies whilst out and about. I pulled out the plastic bag, and the monkey suddenly became very interested in what I was doing, so interested that he almost disappeared inside my backpack. I managed to pass the video camera to Antonio and he then filmed me first of all gently feeding the monkey cashew nuts, through to almost fighting it off to stop it eating the polythene bag holding the nuts. "Fight" was probably too strong a word as we were just playing, but very soon the other tourists gathered around to watch the "show". Although when he nibbled he didn't have sharp teeth, he soon tore a hole in the cashew bag and Fabio had to extricate him from my arms as I was fighting a losing battle keeping the plastic from him. Once the monkey was away from me, I tipped the few remaining cashews into my hand and pocketed the plastic bag swiftly, and then fed him the left over treats. It was just great playing with wild monkeys and it made me think of Gorillas in the Mist on a miniature scale. Although I had been scared of creepy crawlies, crocs and piranhas I was in my element with the monkeys. I just couldn't believe that I'd got so close to them, to be able to play with them. It made me realise just how much I missed not having Misty around anymore.

After leaving the monkey beach, we walked to a small holding not far from the Eco Resort. It was owned and run by a little old lady of about seventy, and she was an amazing person. She used to live further away, then her house had burnt down, killing one of her six daughters. She acquired the piece of land she had now and rebuilt her farm effectively by herself (she was also a widow at this point) while raising the children and fighting off predators. She used to have a couple of dogs but anacondas attacked them both. Apparently the lady was so incensed that she rushed out with a machete and killed the snakes (on two separate occasions). She kept the skins and rolled them out for us. They were about ten feet long each. Antonio said he'd been there once when a snake attacked one of her chickens, and he recounted that she just grabbed the machete, ran outside and sliced the snake in half.

We were shown around the farm, but it was little more than a bit of scrubland with some very old-fashioned equipment and a rickety wooden hut. However, the ingenuity of some of the equipment was pretty impressive, for example, she had fixed up parts of an old bicycle to help mill grain. The kitchen was a three-sided hut with a well used stone oven and a few shelving boards displaying the bare minimum of cooking and eating utensils. But clearly this woman was a survivor. One of her grandsons now lived with her to help her farm, but even so it was a very tough existence. She was given left over food from the Eco resort to help survive, and, in return for this, she allowed the guides to bring people to look around her home and farm, to see how the natives really lived. She had a few knick-knacks for sale and I gave her twenty Reals for a necklace that I knew I would never wear.

I declined going out on another croc expedition that evening, and chose to have an early night after dinner and a catch-up with the diary. Unfortunately the air conditioning wasn't working in my room, however if it was anything like the previous nights, when the temperature dropped outside I wouldn't need it, so I crawled under the covers and drifted off.

Passing Though Buenos Aires: December 30th

The temperatures didn't drop last night and I was awake at 23:00, 00:00, 01:00, 02:00 etc and hardly got any sleep at all. I felt drained. I'd even opened the window to try and get some air through, which was incredibly brave considering the creepy crawly risk (even though there was netting over the hole), but of course it would have to be a totally still night when my air conditioning failed.

I packed up my suitcase, again - not that I'd really unpacked it, and left it outside my hut door and headed down, to breakfast and to settle my bill. Now, remember the four hours getting money changed in Natal? Well, I would have expected it to be much more complicated in the back of beyond. The previous day I'd wanted to change some sterling to pay for the massage. I went to reception, the guy phoned up, presumably, a bank in Manaus and asked what their rate for sterling was - 4.6, the best yet and he just changed the money without even any paperwork or commission. The whole thing took less than two minutes. When I want to settle my bill I had to pay $40 to cover an optional morning tour of Manaus, plus expenses whilst at the hotel, before being taken to the airport,. I asked if they would take two, $20 dollar traveller's checks for the trip and I'd pay the rest in cash. No problem whatsoever. I just countersigned the traveller's cheques, wrote my passport number on the back and the clerk just popped them in the drawer, yet to change money through the Banco do Brasil took four hours and cost me $20 for the pleasure.

We took one of the double-decker boats to Manaus for the morning tour before catching our flights. It was not an especially interesting city to visit, and we only stopped off at the opera house and the municipal market. I could imagine that for anyone who hadn't experienced an Asian market it may have been a bit of an experience, but it was just like any other – bustling with local goods on sale, different herbs and spices etc. However, I never fail to enjoy meandering through local markets, hearing foreign chatter and examining the local varieties of produce, and this one was huge with dedicated meat, fish and vegetable areas, so I did enjoy the walk. The opera house was a resplendent pink building with a gorgeous patterned plaza in front of it.

On the way to the airport Antonio asked the driver to pull over to the side of the road and he reached behind him to pull out a large sack. He opened the car door, gave it to a woman standing on the corner, then got back in and we drove off. He turned to face us,

"My wife. I have to get my laundry done somewhere!" He blew her a kiss as we drove off.

Then to the airport. The other English couple were going to Rio so they could check-in straight away, but my flight hadn't been called yet. I said to the English couple that I'd see them at the other side, and told Antonio he didn't need to hang around for me as I'd be OK. We shook hands farewell, slapped each other on the back and I wished him good luck with his website. I also tipped him pretty well as he had been an extraordinary guide, and I would recommend anyone wanting to visit the Amazon region to look him up. This had been the most wonderful part of my holiday and I was extremely sad to be leaving the Amazon.

As they weren't checking in my flight, and I was feeling a little hungry I decided to buy a chocolate bar to keep me going. It was a large Nestlé Crunch, it was milk chocolate but with the heat and sitting in a glass cabinet for goodness knows how long, it was difficult to consider it anything but white chocolate. That of course made me thirsty so I had to find where I could get a coffee. There were two possibilities, one at each end of the concourse. I chose the wrong end, the one that was closed, but what the hell, they weren't even checking in the flight yet.

After the coffee, I proceeded to see what the check-in situation was like. After nearly missing the flight in Brasilia I was keeping a close eye on the clock. I had to join a queue, which then didn't move for over an hour. The Brazilians amazed me. They seemed to leave everything until the last minute and just when you thought that you were going to be late, you were called to the gate, loaded on quickly and the flight left on time. It was only half an hour before the flight by the time I got checked in, and there was still a fair queue behind me, yet the flight left on time.

I must have had "kid" magnet written all over me as there were eight children surrounding me, two of which were babies, and the flight was hell. It was three and a half hours long and the children were running around, climbing over seats and screeching as they played. I took out my walkman and headphones and found the loudest music I had and turned the volume to full, but even at that amplification, I could hear the baby across the way creating havoc,

137

screaming and squawking at three hundred decibels. I couldn't decide whether the Brazilian kids were the most badly behaved in the world, the least disciplined or both, but most of the internal flights had held "problems" for me. Even across the aisle, the mother who was in between breastfeeding, was shaking a rattle and running it up and down the ribbed side of the drop-down tables as if it were a washer board being used as an instrument. I muttered under my breath, even though nobody would have understood me, "For Christ sake woman; this is a public airline flight!"

As if to add insult to injury, the food was pretty disgusting, so if you are ever taking a Varig flight, I suggest you take a packed lunch with you. I therefore arrived in Sao Paulo in not the best of spirits. I had nearly three hours before my flight to Buenos Aires. There was one in an hour, but I guess the travel agent hadn't wanted to risk a late arrival and a missed connection. In any case, I know Alejandro would be waiting for me, so there was no point in trying to see if I could bring the flight forward.

This check in queue didn't look too bad and all was running smoothly until I reached the counter and was asked for one hundred and eight Reals airport tax. That was the second time I'd been stung for airport tax, and I still had my final exit from Argentina to look forward to.

I didn't have enough cash, so I passed over my credit card, but they needed me to type in my pin number and I didn't know it. As I'd just had my cards replaced following the theft in Budapest, I hadn't received my new pin numbers. In most places this hadn't been a problem as they'd been able to run me off an old-fashioned paper

138

copy to sign, but sadly not at the airport. So, I had to follow the Tam airlines lady over to the Tam info desks. They were not able to help as they no longer used the paper version. The woman then said that I'd have to go and get some money from the machine or change some sterling at the Cambio. I did this by changing £20 at the Cambio, being charged $5 for the pleasure, and returned to the desk and eventually got checked in.

Yet again I had time to spare so I bought some stamps from the post office to post the batch of cards I'd written in the Amazon but had been unable to send because I couldn't get stamps. I purchased some cough mixture and throat lozenges as I felt a cold coming on, and then suddenly I had the munchies again and bought the first ice cream of the holiday.

The actual flight to Buenos Aires was OK, once I'd changed my seat because the back on the allocated seat was broken and kept flopping backwards, and Tam airlines food was significantly better than that offered by Varig. I also had a glass of red wine as my nerves were somewhat frayed by this long journey and the many flight changes to get from Manaus back to Buenos Aires.

As if my day was destined to become increasingly worse as each minute passed, immigration was a nightmare. A plane had landed before ours so the queue was horrendous, however, when I eventually got through, Alejandro was waiting for me at the other side. He said I looked very well and was pleased that I'd made it back to Buenos Aires in one piece. By this time it was 01:30, hardly worth going to the hotel and there were no hotels near the airport because, as Alejandro said, it's a "terminal city" (an unfortunate turn of phrase) as people don't usually just "pass through". So there was a further half hour drive to the city centre, to a cheaper hotel than the one I'd stayed in at the beginning of the holiday.

The hotel looked grim from the outside, but was very nice once inside. Yippee, I had Internet access again. I'd written a batch of mails whilst in the Amazon, knowing that I wouldn't be able to send them until now, and I logged on to find thirty-four emails waiting for me. There was one from George, panicking because he hadn't heard from me for five days. Part of me thought it was nice to have someone "looking out for me" but mainly I was irritated. He knew I was going to the Amazon and I'd said I'd probably be incommunicado whilst there, so there was no need to panic. I didn't know him that well and found his email somewhat "over the top".

Despite the late, or rather early hour, I couldn't switch off my brain, I hadn't seen or heard any news for several days so I logged on to the BBC website intending to have a quick scan and catch up. There was really only one item of news, and I just couldn't believe that all of his had happened whilst I was out of touch for such a relatively short amount of time. There had been a massive tsunami in Asia. They were talking about nearly one quarter of a million people killed. This was a disaster on a scale I had never known before, the pictures almost too surreal to comprehend. Not just the number of estimated deaths and displacements, but the sheer geographic size of the event, impacting Indonesia, Sri Lanka, India, Thailand and Burma, to mention just the main countries. What suddenly made it feel very real was some footage of waves thrashing again Vivekananda Rock Memorial in Tamil Nadu, the plaza totally submerged in water, the same plaza where only six years early, Joe and I had stood for photographs.

I turned the television on, four days after the cataclysmic events, and the news was totally dominated by rising casualties, towns decimated, villages wiped off the face of the earth. Footage of different areas as the Tsunami had hit the coast. The scale was just too large to comprehend. The only other piece of breaking news that was coming in was a fire in the Republica Cromanon nightclub in Buenos Aires, where up to two hundred people were feared dead. The report believed that It had been started by revellers letting off fireworks inside the venue, and owing to curtains and coverings being flammable material, the place had rapidly turned into a fireball. Even worse, most of the emergency exits were chained shut and reporters hypothesised that this was to stop people trying to get in for free. The victims had been burned, suffocated or stampeded to death, and it had happened that evening as I arrived in the very same city.

I went to bed. It was 03:00, but I didn't sleep.

Patagonia: December 31st

I got out of bed at 06:00, realising that I had only had about six hours sleep in the past forty eight hours, and my brain was still buzzing with the world news.

Alejandro collected me at 07:00 to take me to the airport.

"Alejandro, I watched the news for the first time in several days, and learned about the Tsunami in Asia. The scale of the disaster is just too huge to take in."

"There was a disaster close to home last night. A fire in a nightclub in this city. They think that one hundred and eighty people were killed and many more injured. Same old story. The fire escapes were locked. Why don't these club owners learn!" I nodded in agreement and he continued, "this happens a lot in South America, but this is the worst nightclub fire for many years, if not ever. The club got its permit to open not long ago, and it didn't even have fire extinguishers. I think some monies changed hands to sign off this permit. I think that many people will go to jail for this." He said it was only about six blocks away from where I was staying, but I had neither seen nor heard anything.

He saved my place in the check-in queue whilst I went to change a little cash for the airport tax. They wouldn't change my traveller's cheques so I just changed £40. I would be able to get some more when I reached Calafate, my next destination.

Unfortunately I couldn't get an aisle seat (my preference) or a window seat, so it meant that I was going to be trapped between two people for the three hour flight.

"I will be back at the airport to meet you when you return one more time to Buenos Aires," Alejandro said before I went to departures.

"Great," I replied, "and please could you do me one favour before I come back? I'd like to go and see a tango show before I go home, are there any that you can recommend?"

"Recommend!" he exclaimed, "there is only one tango show in Buenos Aires that you have to see, and that is at the Esquina Carlos Gardel. The Carlos Gardel theatre. Carlitos, he invented the Tango. Died so young and tragically in an airplane accident. Thankfully, his music lives on. Yes, I'll get you a ticket for a show at his theatre. They do a special deal - dinner and the show. Do you want to have dinner there also?"

"Yes please. I may as well make an evening of it."

With this I shook his hand and turned towards departures, his final words ringing in my ears.

"Don't forget the rules Suzanne. You must stay in the airport until I find you when you come back. I can't lose you on your last day. The rules Suzanne, remember the rules." I turned and smiled at him.

The flight wasn't "too bad". I found myself sitting next to the same chap I'd been sitting next to on the flight from Sao Paulo. He hadn't gone to a hotel, sensible person, and had just slept at the airport. I fell asleep but was constantly woken by these horrendous throaty snores. It wasn't until about halfway through the flight that I realised it was me! As I was trapped between two people I could only sleep with my head back, and that made me snore. Oh, how awfully embarrassing, but at least I wouldn't have to see any of these people again.

Calafate airport was miniscule. The guide was waiting for me and she asked me to wait outside the terminal. Wow – was it cold! Perhaps not by UK standards, as it was about 15 degrees, but after two weeks at between 30 and 40 degrees, it felt like the Antarctic.

The journey to the hotel took about half an hour, and we passed through Calafate town which was also minuscule, with one main street and a few houses dotted about. The appearance was a cross between a Swiss alpine village and a wild west outpost. It would be a village or very small town in England. The terrain though was the most noticeable as it was a total contrast to the Amazon. There were virtually no trees, and it was very barren and flat. The air though, felt very clean and pure and I sucked at it greedily. It was refreshing in more ways than one to have left the humidity behind.

The hotel was a small hostelry, quite comfortable and about two miles outside the town. Once I'd checked in and handed over some desperately needed laundry, I walked to the town to change some money at the bank (which I had noticed when we drove through) and hopefully to buy a jumper or coat. Guess what, the time was then about 14:00 and the banks had closed at 12:00 because it was

New Year's Eve. Never had I had a holiday so blighted by the difficulty of getting money changed. It would never happen again.

There were a couple of camping shops, but I didn't really want to buy an anorak or parka, but something typically Patagonian. There were only two shops that sold such garments and after much thinking I bought a wool cardigan from one shop and a thick brushed cotton jacket from the other. I saw one really stunning and unusual jacket, and was momentarily tempted, however it was not only extremely expensive but also dirty from the dust blown into the shop. Furthermore I was cautious about buying something that looked like even dry cleaning it may be a challenge with all the different fabrics woven in.

I trekked back the two miles to the hotel with my goodies, stopping en route to grab some ingredients to make myself a sandwich.

Back in the room I had a tortuous time logging on to the Internet. Patagonia obviously had very dodgy telephone lines. I eventually got connected and had a few emails to pick up. I had an email from my dad asking if I was OK because they'd heard about the Buenos Aires fire and knew I was in South America, but not sure exactly where and when. Rather irreverently I laughed to myself, despite the concern he had shown, as one of the sentences read "*and wondered if you'd gone clubbing in Buenos Aires*". I detested nightclubs, and had done so since leaving my teens behind. Without exaggeration, even the thought of walking past a nightclub still brings on an anxiety attack. It's the boom boom boom of an

146

overloud bassline that makes my toes curl. I did, however, drop him a brief email to let him know I was ok.

The news channel on the local TV station had nothing but the Buenos Aires fire, and I was shocked to see close-ups of the dead and dying bodies. You'd never have had such graphic detail back home. It was really quite distressing, and with the Latin temperament, the grief on those gathered around the nightclub was most evident and overwhelming.

I bathed and dressed in the one dress I'd taken with me ready for the hotel's New Year's Eve dinner. It was only a small restaurant, and there were six "romantic couples", three families and me. I was the only English person there. The dinner started at 21:30 and it was still daylight outside, indeed daylight pretty much remained until 23:00. Most bizarre for New Year's Eve. I had a stack of postcards to wish friends Happy New Year from Patagonia and wrote them whilst I was eating. There was part of me that wanted to remain alone and a part that wished that one of the other groups would see I was by myself and ask me to join them. They didn't.

I was feeling pretty okay about things. I had a great view out of the window to the sparse landscape, and there was piped accordion music in the background. I reflected on how I'd spent the last few New Year's Eves. I may have gone out earlier and called on friends, but was always home for at least 23:45 and seen New Year in with Misty. I suddenly missed her enormously, and could picture myself with a glass of champagne or wine, or once even a cup of coffee, toasting her happy New Year. It suddenly turned my mood melancholic, and I resolved that I wasn't going to wait until midnight in the restaurant. I returned to my room about 23:30. I tried to think positively about the year ahead. I'd received a number of emails that said that 2005 would be the year of Rogers International or similar. There was a lot of emotional support and good wishes for me. Suddenly I had yearnings to go home. I'd had enough of the holiday, enough of eating alone, enough of the inner loneliness I managed to suppress most of the time, and I just want my familiar, homely things around me. I wanted to play Sparky.

Of course I realised that I was also extremely tired, and that the cold symptoms I'd been fighting off, the clogged up head and runny nose, were indeed turning into a cold, so it was no surprise that I was feeling a little low. I wanted to hug Cassoulet Ted, my favourite teddy bear that had been a gift from Joe. It all felt very weird. In some ways the three weeks has whizzed past, yet it seemed like months since I was at Iguazu counting the rainbows as the water thundered down the waterfalls.

I had half a dozen or so "Happy New Year" emails I wanted to send, and it took me about twenty five attempts to get connected, but eventually I managed it and they were sent. I glanced at my watch and it was 00:15. I wished myself a happy New Year and fell asleep instantly.

From Jungle to Icebergs: January 1st 2005

Any wobbles from the previous evening were swiftly blown away as I opened my curtains to the most beautiful blue skies and dramatic scenery. What a spectacular vista to start off the New Year, and it made me feel remarkably positive, even though I had a streaming cold.

The itinerary for the day was to see the Perito Moreno Glacier. The coach picked me up at around 11:00 and I set off with my lunch bag that had been provided by the hotel.

The scenery was dactylic. Low, undulating scrubland with the snow capped mountains in the background. The lakes we passed were viridian and aquamarine. Colours I'd never seen in water. My thoughts were interrupted by the guide.

"Today we are going to see the Perito Moreno glacier. I will tell you how this glacier is formed. In areas where there is snow all of the time, layer upon layer of snow is built up. This is compressed into ice and eventually with the weight it re-crystallises. The pressure of the weight of ice and snow forces the glaciers down the mountains, and at the leading edge, the ice breaks off into the rivers. With global warming, many glaciers are melting further up their mountain path and are therefore receding. Perito Moreno though, is affected less than the others."

The drive took us along the banks of Lake Argentina into "Los Glacieares Nacional Park". The colour of Lake Argentina was an amazing turquoise blue, and was the most beautiful lake I had ever seen. As if reading my thoughts the guide continued,

"If you look to the left you will see Lake Argentina. The lovely colour is due to the various minerals in the ice blocks, being released into the water as the icebergs melt."

As we entered the National Park, trees started to appear. The Perito Moreno glacier rolls towards a little island. Sometimes it reaches the island and then a tunnel is formed by the water being at different heights at either side of the blockage. The water then seeps through, forms a stream, the tunnel collapses and the formation starts all over again.

The first sighting of the glacier was a truly majestic panorama, with its cliff edge being an average of one hundred metres high, and the accumulation area, the part of a glacier that is perennially covered with snow, stretching miles into the distance between the mountains. We all climbed down from the coach to take photos and then we wended our way down a narrow road to the waterside, where we boarded a boat to go and see the south face of the glacier. We passed a few small icebergs, which I photographed with gusto as I'd never seen an iceberg before, however I very quickly realised that these were nothing more than flotsam, because the closer we got to the glacier, the larger these icebergs became, some the size of a small ocean liner. They were mainly white, as of course I'd expected, however I hadn't realised just how many shades of blue would be reflected off them, nor how jagged some of their spires were.

The boat went right up to the terminus of the glacier and stayed there for around twenty minutes so that we could study, watch and photograph the landscape. Blocks of ice brake away from glaciers, varying in size, from small pieces to huge boulders, This is called calving, and once I started looking for them I became entranced. There were pieces jutting out, looking as if they were hanging on precariously and I just stared at them hoping to see them snap off. There was one huge promontory hanging over an ice cave, and it looked like any second it would come crashing down, but it didn't whilst I was watching it. There would be a rumble and cracking sound and another piece of ice would come crashing down, and I'd turn to see where it was coming from but invariably it would hit the water before I had time to aim the camera.

After the boat trip we drove to the north facing side of the glacier for a different view. I was extremely impressed by it even though I wasn't feeling at all well with the cold, possibly because it was the first one I'd seen. Although changing from one temperature zone to another may have had an impact, I was sure that breathing in other's germs during the numerous flights to get here, was the main culprit.

We alighted the boat and stayed at the north facing side for a couple of hours. There are paths down the mountainside so that you could see the glacier from different angles. Every now and then a piece of glacier split away, and my ears became attuned to the creaking and splintering sound followed by a whoosh.

151

Most bizarrely it reminded me of an old amusement arcade game. The penny fountains, where you drop a penny in the slot and there are moving platforms below with pennies mounting up, and you know, yes, you just know, that the next penny you drop will push the mountain of coins over the edge and you will win the jackpot. Watching glaciers crack is the same. You see a piece that you are absolutely certain is about to crash into the river, but nothing happens. Indeed the piece you are looking at probably won't splinter off for a couple of weeks, but you are mesmerized into staring at it, willing it to drop off in front of you.

Back to the hotel where I dined on steak. Yep, back in Argentina, so the diet returned to succulent beef. I then dosed myself up with various cold remedies and crashed out.

More Icebergs: January 2nd

The tour promised a full day out to the Napala glacier and some other smaller ones. I didn't especially feel like going as my cold was no better. Furthermore, now I'd see one glacier, and an extremely impressive one at that, I wasn't that interested in seeing any more. Don't get me wrong, I didn't regret flying all the way down to Patagonia to witness this example of nature's beauty, but I decided that glaciers weren't really my thing. I much preferred the jungle, and having witnessed the king of glaciers, I knew that the smaller ones wouldn't have the same stunning impact.

The coach pick up was at 07:45 and then there was a half hour drive to where we picked up the boat for the cruise.

It was quite a large boat compared to the one the previous day, about the size of an English Channel ferry, and it was packed like the proverbial sardines. They constantly repeated over tannoy that once you had a seat you have to retain it for the whole journey. I was okay with my seat until I realised that I had the world's worst sniffer in front of me, an Argentinean who "snort sniffed" on average every forty seconds. It was disgusting and yet I seemed to be the only person fazed by it. You may have realised now that the common denominator between my dislike of children, nightclubs and sniffers is the sound. I have an exceptionally low noise tolerance level. I buried my head in my latest book only emerging to pop out on deck occasionally to see an iceberg or admire the scenery. Unfortunately it was bitterly cold and, as I didn't have full winter gear with me, it was just too cold to stay out there for long periods, despite getting away from sniffer.

We passed some gargantuan icebergs and I found them more fascinating and picturesque than the little glaciers. Blue has always been my favourite colour, and, of the different shades, forget-me-not blue was at the top, however I decided that iceberg blue came a very close second.

Halfway through the day we stopped, alighted from the boat and could walk through a sparse woodland to a lake. For me that was the highlight of the day as the lake was teeming with little icebergs. Luckily out in the forest I could break away from the other visitors and have some peace alone, just looking and taking in the scenery and being present with myself for the moment.

One thing that struck me about the national park was how clean it was. We were told numerous times that we had to take rubbish away with us, that you couldn't throw anything into the water and so on, but back in England people would still have littered the place, but here there wasn't a single crisp packet or coke can anywhere. It was absolutely clean and free from rubbish. The air was so fresh that you could taste it, and the cold burned the back of my throat. It did feel a little strange that only forty hours previously, I'd been in the Amazon jungle, yet here I was in the bitter cold, in a totally different landscape, looking at icebergs.

We didn't get back to the hotel until around 20:00 so I went straight into dinner for another steak. The menu was quite simple but the food excellent. It would be the equivalent of superior farmhouse cooking in the UK.

The TV was unbelievable. The local news channel was still showing clips from the nightclub fire and the cameramen zooming in on the dead and badly injured bodies. It must have been horrendous if you were a relative or friend watching this footage. Also on the evening news a car had exploded at a petrol station killing two people and injuring several more, again the cameraman zoomed in on the totally mangled car with pools of blood and bits of body. Argentineans must have strong stomachs to watch their news every day.

I tried to get connected again, but to no avail and ditto when I try the hotel computer. Oh well, I'd have to wait until I got back to Buenos Aires the next day, for the last day of the holiday.

A Tango Show to Remember: January 3rd

Due to the fifteen kilos weight restrictions on internal flights, I reduced my suitcase to the minimum weight, discarding everything I possibly could - such as leaving books I'd read in the room, and putting all the heavy things in my small backpack for carry-on luggage. It was a shame really when the next day I would have a full forty kilos allowance. I reckoned it was a close call as to whether my backpack was heavier than my suitcase. Unfortunately, as I was packing the stone accordion man I felt that something had crumbled and was definitely broken inside the package. I poked the top open and could see that his head had come off and his hat had broken into a couple of places – damn. I couldn't be bothered to unpack the whole thing, so left it to examine properly when I got to Buenos Aires where I would make the call whether to ditch him, if he was too badly broken, or take him home and glue him back together.

At check out, they were having a problem with my bill and they just didn't believe it as there appeared to be a lot of phone charges, indeed four pages of them. Of course it was all the times I tried to get connected and the minimum charge for just picking up the phone was two Reals. I explained that I had been trying to get connected to the internet, and the receptionist asked me whether I succeeded. Once I replied. She then took off all the two Real charges and just left me those where I got half connected before it had cut out. I thought that that was very decent of them, as they didn't have to do that, and I hadn't even asked them to. It was a lovely little hotel and they had looked after me exceptionally well.

Back to the miniscule airport for my tenth flight of the holiday and back to Buenos Aires where Alejandro was to meet me. He said that he felt he knew me really well because of all the times he'd met me at the airport, I gave him one of my "Susan Rogers Accordionist" cards which had my phone number and email address, and told him that if he ever came to the UK to let me know, and I'd meet him at the airport. I was also back to Loi Suites Recoletta, the first hotel I stayed in, so I'd truly come in a full circle.

I negotiated with reception to do two pieces of laundry on express - my chinos and a polo shirt. They agreed, but of course there be would a surcharge.

I dumped my stuff in the room, changed into shorts and flip-flops for the last time, and made my way to my first port of call, the Cambio. I reckoned that I could write a tourist guide to getting money changed in South America. The other book I'd thought of writing was a directory of where you can get a free breakfast all over the world. I had this idea a couple of years previously when travelling on business, and noted the number of hotels that didn't ask you for your room number when you had breakfast. I had this theory that so long as you looked like you "could" be stopping at the hotel, you would get a free breakfast. The book remains unwritten.

The Cambio took a little longer than usual because of the queue but I then wandered over to my favourite café for a last beer and ice cream followed by a stroll through Recoletta market where I bought a couple of wooden dangly things for my conservatory. It was also my last opportunity to admire (ogle?) this most handsome of races. How could one country have them all?

Back in the room, I logged on for the first time in a few days and read New Year greetings from several people. There was an especially lovely email from Joe:

Dear Susan

Happy New Year to you too - and I really mean that. You deserve to find, not only happiness, but contentment (although I am not sure if you would be comfortable with 'contentment' because it has an element of resignation in it). God only knows (if he exists) you work hard enough to find happiness and some kind of mental peace. You have faced so much in 2004 but you are a brave and talented lady and 2005, while likely being your biggest (but not the bravest) challenge, I believe will bring you your greatest rewards. I just got in and wanted to get this off quickly in case you logged on during your travels .

Joe

It actually made me cry. I was so lucky to have such a fantastic friend.

I sent my last batch of "Greetings from Buenos Aires" emails, telling everyone that I had completed my nearly 10,000 miles circuit of Brazil and Argentina and would be on my way home the next day.

I tipped out the suitcase and re-packed everything tightly, getting everything in except what I'd need for my final flight home. I inspected my stone man, and although a piece from his hat had actually crumbled to dust, I knew that I could glue him back together when I got home, and the small missing piece from his hat would just make him look more rustic.

As Alejandro had managed to get me a ticket, it was off to the Tango show at the Carlos Gardel theatre. I was shown to my place on a long trestle type table, and told that I could choose a starter, main course and dessert from a limited set menu. It was all a bit "conveyor belt like", however the theatre was full and they had a lot of people to serve food to before the show started. Drink was included and the waiter kept topping me up with red wine. Whilst eating and waiting for the show to commence there was a movie telling the history of the tango. It was in Spanish with English subtitles and I hadn't realised that it was a relatively new musical development and only came about circa 1920.

Just my luck, but sitting opposite me was a kid about eight years old who kept kicking me under the table. Initially I thought it was accidental, however as our eyes met, I realised that it wasn't. I moved my legs, but he then stretched his out and continued to kick me. I tried to resist a confrontation, but in the end, reached under the table and, whack, I slapped his legs. He immediately feigned tears and turned to his mother babbling. I leaned over to her and said in Spanish that I didn't speak much Spanish but -she interrupted me and said that she spoke English. I told her that her son had been kicking me under the table, and although I'd given him the eye to stop, he'd continued until I slapped his leg. She turned to him and questioned him, and then turned to me and said that he hadn't realised that he was kicking my legs - yeah, but she

160

was very sorry and she swapped places with him. She knew that he knew, and I knew that she knew that he knew. It transpired that she was with a group of Mexicans on holiday and we chatted quite affably after that.

The Tango show was excellent. The music was provided by a Piazzola type sextet and the different artists performed solo dances, group dances and singing. I especially enjoyed the bandoneon solo, allegedly the most difficult instrument to learn to play. There was extremely passionate dancing and I noticed how they caressed each other in the most gentle and subtle of touches, yet in the most seductive of ways. For example, the man when putting his arm around the woman, would let the very tip of his fingers gently caress across the underside of her breasts.

Most of the men were young and dressed in black, but there was one older guy, probably in his early sixties and dressed in white, and the crowd went wild when he came on stage. The Mexican lady leaned across and said that he was one of the most famous tango dancers in Argentina. It was absolutely fascinating to watch, because this guy was not in the least good looking. He was dapper, balding on top, the rest of his hair greased back and was definitely not of the same calibre of men I'd been ogling earlier. He was also somewhat shorter than his tall, young and elegant dance partner. But my God, could he dance. Every single movement of his body exuded sexiness. Even a little twitch of a finger. It was stunning to watch, and what totally made it for me was that he danced to La Cumparsita, one of my favourite tangos and one I played on the accordion. Throughout the routine there was hushed silence throughout the auditorium, and then when they completed the dance everyone rose to their feet with a giant roar of appreciation. I felt humbled to have been lucky enough to witness this performance.

I didn't get back to the hotel until around 01:00. My laundry hadn't reappeared, so I went down to reception to enquire. They asked if I could wait until the morning, but as I was paying express charges I said no, I needed it then, and made them find it. The pieces were ready, but the trousers had obviously been ironed in a hurry as they had more ironed in crinkles than they had before they went in. Oh well, at least I wouldn't smell on the plane.

Homeward Bound: January 4th

The last day. I was up, washed, breakfasted and ready by 07:30. Alejandro wasn't coming for me until 10:00, so a chance to have one last stroll around La Recoletta.

I loved Buenos Aires very much, and I hoped to get back again at some point in the future. To this day, it remains my favourite city in the world.

Alejandro was of course on time and off we went to the airport. Check-in was extremely painless, because I was returning in business class, so there were only two people in the queue in front of me. I mentioned the news reports and that I found them quite disturbing with their graphic detail and Alejandro said that it was the normal way they reported accidents and disasters.

"Suzanne, I hope that you liked the show last night?"

"Absolutely, It was a great evening and the dancing was exquisite. I had an incident with a young kid kicking my legs, but we sorted that out and I ended up chatting to his mother and her friends during the evening. The most stunning dance was performed by an old chap at the end of the show. I'd just never experienced anything like it, and the audience obviously loved him because they went wild at the end. It was a shame that he only did one dance."

"Ah – he is a maestro. Not only is he one of the most famous tango dancers in Argentina but he also does the choreography for the troupe you saw. He now only dances once at the end of the show, but people still love him."

"I can understand that. He was memorising"

I said farewell to Alejandro and promised to send him an email when I get home as he said he wanted to make sure that I arrived safely

The flight home was awful with six kids in business class running amok and squealing. Luckily, and for a change, there was a hostess who wasn't afraid to have a word with the parents. Apparently, one of the reasons two of the kids were running around was that their mother was in first class and she'd dumped the kids in business class with their father and they kept running through the plane to see her. Unbelievable!

I managed to get a few hours sleep though, so not too bad I guess.

Epilogue: January 5th

I was home, and it was cold, damp and a bitter wind was blowing up. I went to Barclays Bank in Wendover at about 14:00 to change the last of my traveller's cheques back to sterling. It was closed. I didn't know, that as a small village bank they only opened from 09:30 to 13:00.................

I burst out laughing!

By the same author:

Vietnam: Journey of Unexpected delights

To find out more about the author, visit:

www.susanrogersauthor.co.uk

To find out more about tours in the Amazon, visit:

www.aguiaamazonas.com.br